Japanese Business Dictionary

Japanese Business Dictionary

Edited by

Ritsuko Moore

Schreiber Publishing
Rockville, Maryland

Japanese Business Dictionary
Morry Sofer, Editor
Ritsuko Moore, Japanese Editor

Published by:

Schreiber Publishing
Post Office Box 4193
Rockville, MD 20849 USA
www.schreiberpublishing.com

First printing

Library of Congress Cataloging-in-Publication Data

Japanese business dictionary / edited by Ritsuko Moore.
p. cm.
ISBN 0-88400-313-0
1. Business--Dictionaries. 2. Commerce--Doctionaries. 3. English language--Dictionarie--Japanese. I. Moore, Ritsuko.

HF1002 .J355 2005
330'. 03--dc22

2005010888

Printed in the United States of America

Introduction

Business language around the world in the twenty-first century is in a state of rapid change. This creates the need for new business dictionaries that are not tied to the past but rather reflect the new global economy. This is particularly true in regard to an English-Japanese business dictionary, which brings together two economic systems that are far from identical. Japan is an economic giant, playing a critical role in the world economy. As one of the business leaders of the world, its business and high tech language evolves rapidly, and requires good linguistic tools to cope with the global economy.

The main corollary of this new reality is that even a new English-Japanese business dictionary is not going to be exhausttive and definitive. But at least it is a start. It is to be expected that such a dictionary will be updated at least once a year or every two years at the most.

Many of the English business terms in this dictionary are very American-specific. As such, they do not always have equivalent terms in Japanese and therefore are explained in some detail.

This dictionary covers many areas of business, such as banking, insurance, real estate, export-import, stock market, and more. In addition, several hundred business-related computer and Internet terms have been included.

Many of the Japanese business terms used today are directly copied from English. Some of the English business terms have both a Japanese term and an English term rendered in a Japanese form. The user of this dictionary is advised not to look upon all the Japanese terms herein included as cast in stone. Some may be questioned by business professionals in Japan. But it goes without saying that the need for this kind of dictionary is urgent and it should go a long way in contributing to better trade relations between English-speaking and Japanese-speaking business partners.

A

abandonment
委託、放棄
abandonment clause
委付条項
abatement
排除、失効
ABC method
ABC 方式
ability to pay
担税力、支払能力
abort
中止（する）、アボート
above the line
一定の標準以上の、
経常支出の
absence rate, absenteeism
欠勤率、常習欠勤、
(地主の）長期不在、
不在地主制度
absentee owner
不在地主、無機能資本家
absolute advantage
絶対優位
absolute liability
絶対責任、無過失責任
absolute sale
無条件売買
absorbed
吸収された、
併合された
absorption costing
全部原価計算
absorption rate
吸収率
abstention
破産回避、（投票の）棄権
abstract of record
登記書
abstract of title
権利証明要約書
abusive tax shelter
税金避難手段の乱用
accelerated cost recovery system (ACRS)
加速原価回収方式
accelerated depreciation
加速償却
acceleration
加速、加速度、促進
acceleration clause
利益喪失条項、弁済期日繰上日条項
accelerator, accelerator principle
加速度因子、
加速度原理
acceptance
受領、手形の引受け
acceptance sampling
受入れ抜き取り検査

access
アクセスする、接続する
accession
登録、受入、符合
access right
アクセス権
access time
アクセスタイム,
呼出し時間
accommodation endorser, maker or party
融通手形裏書人、
融通手形振出人
accommodation paper
融通手形
accord and satisfaction
代物弁済
account
会計、勘定、計算書, 口座、
報告（書）、説明、理由、
評価、利益
accountability
執行責任、職責
accountancy
会計業務、会計学、
会計制度
accountant
会計士、計理士
accountant's opinion
会計士の意見
account executive
アカウント・
エグゼクティブ、
顧客会計主任
accounting change
会計方針変更
accounting cycle
会計周期
accounting equation
会計等式
accounting error
会計ミス
accounting method
会計方法、会計手続き
accounting period
会計期間、会計年度
accounting principles, accounting standards
会計原則、会計基準
accounting procedure
会計手続き
accounting rate of return
会計的利益率
accounting records
会計帳簿、会計記録
accounting software
財務会計ソフト
accounting system
会計システム、
会計制度
account number
課金番号、勘定番号
accounts payable
買掛金、未払金
accounts payable ledger
仕入先元帳
accounts receivable
売掛金（勘定）
受取勘定

accounts receivable financing
売掛金担保融資
accounts receivable ledger
得意先元帳
accounts receivable turnover
売掛金回転率
account statement
計算書、
預金取引明細書
accredited investor
公認投資家
accretion
増大、増加物、付加価値、
価値増加
accrual method
発生主義
accrue
利子がつく
accrued interest
未払利息、未払利子
accrued liabilities
未払債務、見越負債
accrued taxes
未収税金、未収租税
accumulated depletion
累積減耗償却
accumulated depreciation
減価償却引当金、
累積減価償却額
accumulated dividend
未払配当、
未払配当金
accumulated earnings tax or accumulated profits
留保収益税、留保利益金
acid test ratio
当座比率
acknowledgment
承認、確認、領収書
acquisition
取得、買収、
（企業の）吸収
acquisition cost
取得原価
acre
エーカー、土地
acreage
エーカー数で計った面積
across the board
一律に、全体的に
activate
起動する
active income
能動所得
activate a file
ファイルを起動する、
ファイルを作動させる
activate a macro
マクロを起動する
active cell
（表計算ソフトの）
アクティブセル
active market
好況市場、好況市況
act of bankruptcy
破産法
act of god
不可抗力、天災

actual cash value
取替え価額、現金換価価値
actual cost
実費、実際原価
actual damages
現実的損害賠償金
actuarial science
数理科学、保険統計科学
actuary
保険数理士
addendum
補遺、付録
additional first-year depreciation (tax)
初年度割増償却（税）
additional mark-on
追加値入、
追加マークアップ
additional paid-in capital
追加払込資本金
add-on interest
アドオン金利
adequacy of coverage
保険担保の妥当性、適用範囲の妥当性
adhesion contract
附合契約、附従契約
adhesion insurance contract
附合保険契約
ad infinitum
無限に、永久に、無限の、永久の
ad item
アド・アイテム、
同じ点について
adjective law
手続形式法
adjoining
近接の、隣接する
adjudication
判決、破産宣告、裁定
adjustable life insurance
調整可能生命保険
adjustable margin
調節可能なマージン（欄外）
adjustable mortgage loan (AML)
調整金利抵当ローン
adjustable-rate mortgage (ARM)
変動金利住宅ローン、
利率変動型抵当
adjusted basis or adjusted tax basis
修正基礎額、
修正課税基準
adjusted gross income
調整済総収入、修正総所得
adjuster
損害（海損）査定人、
海損精算人
adjusting entry
修正仕分、修正記入
administer
経営する、管理する
administered price
管理価格
administrative expense
経営費、管理費

administrative law
行政法
administrative management society
経営管理学会
administrative services only (ASO)
行政職種限定、一般管理サービスのみ
administrator
行政官、管理人、管財人
administrator's deed
遺産管理人の捺印証書 **ad valorem**
価格に従って、
価格に準じた
advance
立替金、前払い
advanced funded pension plan
事前積立年金制度
adversary
相手方、
相手方当事者
adverse opinion
反対意見
adverse possession
不法占有
advertising
広告、広告業
advertising appropriation
広告費、
広告充当金
affective behavior
感情的行動
affidavit
（宣誓）供述書、口述書、宣誓書
affiliated chain
チェーン加盟店
affiliated company
従属会社、関連会社
affiliated retailer
関連小売業者、
加盟小売業者
affirmative action
アファーマティブ·
アクション、
マイノリティー優遇措置
affirmative relief
被告に与えられる救済
after-acquired clause
事後取得条項
after-acquired property
事後取得財産
after market
アフターマーケット、
第二次市場
after-tax basis
税引後ベース
after-tax cash flow
税引キャッシュフロー
after-tax real rate of return
税引後実質利回り
against the box
空売りで
age discrimination
年齢差別
agency
代理店、（政府の）機関

agency by necessity
必要代理店
agent
代理人、代理店
agglomeration
集団、アグロメレーション
agglomeration diseconomies
集団の不経済性
aggregate demand
総需要
aggregate income
総所得
aggregate indemnity (aggregate limit)
総責任限度額、
総損害賠償限度額
aggregate supply
総供給
aging of accounts receivable or aging schedule
売掛金の経過期間調査または経過期間表
agreement
合意（書）、契約（書）
agreement of sale
売買契約
agribusiness
アグリビジネス、
農業関連産業
air bill
航空貨物輸送状
airfreight
航空貨物（の）、
空輸する
air rights
空中権
aleatory contract
偶発事契約、射倖契約
alienation
割譲、譲渡、疎外
alien corporation
外国企業
alimony
別居手当、離婚手当
allegation
申立て、陳述
allocate
割り当てる、
配分する
allocated benefits
表定給付
allocation of resources
資源配分
allodial
自由保有地の、
完全私有地の
allodial system
私有地制度
allowance
割当額、手当、給与、
割引
allowance for depreciation
減価償却引当金
allowed time
有給時間、許容時間
all risk/all peril
全危険担保の
alternative hypothesis
対立仮説、代替仮説
alternative minimum tax
中低所得層税減免の１つ

alternative mortgage instrument (AMI)
代替抵当手段
amass
蓄積する、集める
amend
修正する、補正する
amended tax return
（税金の）修正申告
amendment
改正、修正（条項）、補正書
amenities
生活を便利にする施設・設備アメニティ
American Stock Exchange (AMEX)
アメリカ株式取引所
amortization
年賦償還、割賦償却（金）
amortization schedule
債務償還計画（表）
analysis
分析、解析
analysis of variance (ANOVA)
分散分析法
analysts
アナリスト、分析者
analytic process
分析過程
analytical review
分析的研究（レビュー）
anchor tenant
アンカーテナント
animate
～を活発にさせる、動かす
annexation
付加物、併合
annual basis
年次ベース、年間ベース
annual debt service
年間未払金サービス
annual earnings
年間所得、年間収入
annual meeting
年次総会、年次会合
annual mortgage constant
年間抵当貸付定数
annual percentage rate (APR)
年率
annual report
年次報告書、年報
annual wage
年間賃金
annuitant
年金受取人、年金受給者
annuity
年金、年金収受権
annuity due
期首払込金
annuity factor
年金係数
annuity in advance
前払い年金
annuity in arrears
未払い年金

answer
解決策、対策
anticipated holding period
予想資産保有期限
anticipatory breach
期限前の契約違反
antitrust acts
独占禁止法,
反トラスト法
antitrust laws
独占禁止法、
反トラスト法
apparent authority
表見的権限
appeal bond
上訴供託金
appellate court (appeals court)
上訴裁判所、控訴裁判所
applet
アプレット
application of funds
資金の運用、資金の使途
application program
アプリケーション
プログラム
application software
アプリケーション
ソフトウエア
application window
アプリケーション
ウィンドウ
applied economics
応用経済学
applied overhead
応用間接費
applied research
応用研究
apportionment
割当、分配、配当
appraisal
評価、（資産の）査定
appraisal rights
鑑定権
appraise
鑑定する
appraiser
鑑定人、（税関の）
査定官
appreciate
価値が上がる、
値上がりする
appreciation
（価格の）騰貴、増加
appropriate
（予算を）計上する、充当
する
appropriated expenditure
特殊割当支出金
appropriation
支出充当、（予算の）
承認、予算割当額
approved list
承認リスト
appurtenant
ーに従属して、
従属している、
他物付属の
appurtenant structures
付属建築
a priori statement
直感的声明、推測的報告書

arbiter
裁決者、仲裁人
arbitrage
鞘取引，鞘売買，裁定取引
arbitrage bond
裁定取引契約、鞘取引約定
arbitration
仲裁、仲裁裁判、裁定
arbitrator
仲裁人
archive storage
アーカイブ・ストレージ、
公文書（保管所）
arm's length transaction
独立当事者間の互いに対等
な立場での取引
array
配列、配列する
arrearage
滞り、未払金、予備に保存
したもの
arrears
滞納、滞納金
articles of incorporation
会社定款
artificial intelligence (AI)
人工知能
as is
現状有姿（で）、現品限り、
正札どおり
asked
請求された、
提示された
asking price
提示価格
assemblage
組立て
assembly line
組立ライン、
アセンブリーライン
assembly plant
組立工場
assess
査定する、賦課する
assessed valuation
鑑定額、査定価額
assessment
賦課（金）、査定（額）
assessment ratio
評価額比率
assessor
(財産)評価人、（課税）査
定人、（損害）鑑定人
asset
資産、資産の一項目
asset depreciation range (ADR)
資産償却限度
assign
譲渡する、割当てる
assignee
譲受人、管財人
assignment
譲渡、譲渡証書
assignment of income
収入を抵当にした借金、
収入譲渡（証書）
assignment of lease
賃借権の譲渡
assignor
譲渡人
assimilation
同化、同化作用、混成作用

association
連合、組合，協会、提携
assumption of mortgage
抵当の引き受け
asterisk
アステリスク、星印
asynchronous
非同期（式）の、異時性の、非同期性、非同期
at par
額面価格で、払込額で、割引なしで、
at risk
危険な状態で、危険にさらされて
attachment
添付書類、差押、差押令状
attained age
現在の年齢
attention
～宛て
attention line
名宛人記載欄、アテンションライン
attest
証言する、証明する、誓言する
at the close
大引けに
at the opening
寄り付き注文
attorney-at-law
弁護士
attorney-in-fact
代理人
attribute sampling
アトリビュートサンプリング
attrition
自然減（耗）、消耗
auction or auction sale
オークション、競売
audience
観客、聴衆、視聴者、聞き手、読者、
audit
会計監査、決算、（会計を）監査する
auditing standards
監査基準
auditor
監査役、会計監査人
auditor's certificate
監査役証明書
auditor's certificate, opinion, or report
監査役証明書、監査意見書、監査（人）報告書
audit program
監査計画、監査計画書
audit trail
監査証跡、監査の手がかり
authentication
（文書）の真正性証明、認証
authorized shares or authorized stock
授権株式数、授権株式
automatic checkoff
自動天引き
automatic (fiscal) stabilizers
自動（財政）安定装置

automatic merchandising
自動販売機による販売

automatic reinvestment
自動再投資

automatic withdrawal
預金自動引出し

auxiliary file
補助ファイル

average
平均（値）、
平均株価

average cost
平均費用

average (daily) balance
平均（一日）残高

average down
難平買い

average fixed cost
平均固定費用

average tax rate
平均税率

avoirdupois
常衡

avulsion
(土地の）自然分離、突然の転位

B

baby bond
少額債券
baby boomers
１945 年から 60 年代に生まれた人、ベビーブーマー、ベビーブーム世代の人
backdating
日付を遡らせること、前の日付けに遡って発効すること
background investigation
背後事情の調査、経歴・履歴調査
background check
背後事情の調査、経歴・履歴調査
back haul
帰路、復路、逆送
backlog
注文残高、売残品
back office
窓際、非営業部門
back pay
未払給料、遡及的給与
backslash
バックスラッシュ、逆スラッシュ
backspace key
バックスペースキー
back up
バックアップ
backup file
バックアップ・ファイル
back up withholding
予備
backward-bending supply curve
後方屈伸供給曲線
backward vertical integration
後方垂直統合
bad debt
不良債権、貸倒金
bad debt recovery
不良債権回復
bad debt reserve
貸倒引当金、貸倒準備金
bad title
欠陥のある権原、不良権原
bail bond
保釈金、保釈保証書
bailee
受託者、受寄者
bailment
寄託、保釈、保釈金
bait and switch advertising
おとり広告、誇大広告
bait and switch pricing
おとり商法的価格設定
balance
差額、差引残高

balanced mutual fund
均衡投資信託
balance of payments
国債収支、支払残高
balance of trade
貿易収支
balance sheet
貸借対照表、
バランスシート
balance sheet reserve
貸借対照表予備金
balloon payment
最終残額一括払い、
バルーン返済、風船式支払
ballot
投票用紙、投票、投票総数
bandwidth
（周波数）帯域幅
bank
銀行、銀行に預ける
banker's acceptance
銀行引受手形
bank holding company
銀行持株会社
bank line
銀行信用供与限度額、
銀行与信限度額
bankruptcy
倒産，破産，破綻
bank trust department
銀行信託部門
bar
弁護士業、弁護士団、法曹（団）、阻却事由
bar code
バーコード、
統一商品コード
bar code label
バーコードラベル
bargain and sale
大安売り、特売
bargain hunter
特売品あさり、割安株狙いの投資家
bargaining agent
交渉代表権者
bargaining unit
交渉単位、
交渉団体
barometer
バロメーター、
指標
barter
物々交換、バーター、
物々交換する
base rate pay
基本給与
base period
基準年次
base rent
基準賃貸料
base-year analysis
基準年次分析
basic input-output system (BIOS)
バイオス、
基本入出力システム
basic limits of liability
基本的責任限度額

basic module
基本モジュール
basic operating system
基本オペレーティング
システム
basis
基礎、基本、基準、原則
basis point
基準ポイント（１％の
１００分の１）
batch application
バッチアプリケーション
batch file
バッチファイル
batch processing
一括処理（作業）
battery
バッテリー、電池
baud
変調速度
baud rate
ボーレート
bear
弱気筋、売方、売りたたく
bearer bond
無記名公債
bear hug
ベアハッグ、
強く抱きしめること
bear market
売相場、弱気市場
bear raid
弱気筋の市場攪乱
bellwether
先導者、先行指標、
先導指数
below par
額面以下で、割り引きで、
benchmark
ベンチマーク、規準点
beneficial interest
受益的権利、（信託の）受
益権
beneficial owner
受益株主、使用収益権者
beneficiary
受益者、（保険金などの）
受取人
benefit
給付金、年金
benefit-based pension plan
手当に基ずく年金制度
benefits, fringe
付加給付、福利厚生給付
benefit principle
利益原則、応益原則
bequeath
遺贈する、遺譲する
bequest
遺贈、遺産
best's rating
格付け会社ベストによる評
価
beta coefficient
ベータ係数
betterment
改良、（不動産の）
価格騰貴
biannual
半期の、年２回の
bid and asked
買呼値と売呼値

bid bond
入札保証状
bidding up
せり上げ
biennial
隔年の、２年に１回の、２年ごとの
big board
ニューヨーク証券取引所
big-ticket items
高価な商品
bilateral mistake
双方過失、
当事者双方による錯誤
bill
手形、勘定書、請求書
billing cycle
支払請求周期、
請求書作成周期
bill of exchange
（外国）為替手形、
輸出手形
bill of landing
船荷証券
binder
仮契約、仮保険証、
手付金
bit error rate
ビット誤り率
bit map
ビットマップ
black list
ブラックリスト
black market
ブラックマーケット、
闇市場、闇取引
blank cell
ブランクセル、空白セル
blanket contract
一括契約、包括的契約
blanket insurance
総合保険、包括保険
blanket mortgage
一括担保、包括的抵当
blanket recommendation
全面的推薦
bleed
赤字を出す
blended rate
混合料率
blended value
混合価額
blighted area
胴枯れ地帯、荒廃地区
blind pool
安全運用委任型資金連合
委任企業同盟
blind trust
白紙委任信託
blister packaging
ブリスター包装
block
ブロック（株券取引単位）
blockbuster
圧倒的な影響力を与える
人・物、
悪徳不動産業者、
立ち退かせ屋
blockbusting
ブロックバスティング、
ブロック破壊商法、
不動産屋の悪徳商法

block policy
包括保険証券、
予定保険証書
block sampling
ブロックのサンプリング、
一区画抜き取り見本
blowout
新規発行債券の即完売、
どんちゃん騒ぎ
度を超す行為
blue-chip stock
花形株
blue collar
ブルーカラー、
肉体労働者
blue laws
清教徒的厳法、日曜厳守法
blueprint
青写真、詳細な計画
blue-sky law
ブルースカイ法、青空法
board of directors
取締役会、役員会、理事会
board of equalization
平等化委員会
boardroom
役員会議室、理事会議室、
立会所
boilerplate
共通記事、
決まり文句、共通条項
bona fide
真実に（の）、真正に
（の）
bona fide purchaser
善意の購買者
bond
債券、公債証書、債務証書
bond broker
債券ブローカー
bond discount
債券割引、社債発行差金
bonded debt
公債発行（による）借入金、
社債発行（による）借入金
bonded goods
保税貨物、保税品
bond premium
社債発行差金、
社債発行プレミアム
bond rating
公社債の格付け
book
会計簿、帳簿
book-entry securities
帳簿記入証券
book inventory
帳簿棚卸
bookkeeper
簿記係、記帳係
bookmark
ブックマーク、しおり
book value
帳簿価額
boondoggle
役に立たない仕事、
無用な仕事をする
boot
利益
boot
(computer)
ブートする、

コンピューターを起動する、
システムを立ち上げる
boot record
起動記録、ブート記録
borrowed reserve
借入準備金
borrowing power of securities
証券借入能力
bottom
底、景気の谷底、市況の底値
bottom fisher
底値株専門に狙う投資家、
ボトムフィッシャー
bottom line
結論、本音、純損益
Boulewarism
ブーレワリズム
（反差別法に関する）
boycott
ボイコット、不買同盟
brainstorming
ブレーンストーミング
branch office manager
支店長
brand
銘柄、商標、品種
brand association
ブランド連想、
ブランド関連
brand development
銘柄開発
brand development index (BDI)
銘柄開発指数
brand extension
ブランド拡充
brand image
商標イメージ、
ブランドイメージ
brand loyalty
ブランド名使用料
brand manager
ブランドマネージャー
brand name
商標名、有名ブランド
brand potential index (BPI)
銘柄潜在性指数
brand share
ブランドシェア、商標占有率
breach
不履行、
（法律・約束などを）破る
breach of contract
契約違反、契約不履行、
協定違反、違約、破約
breach of warranty
保証違反、保証不履行
breadwinner
（一家の）稼ぎ手、財源
break
急激な変化、
相場の暴落
break-even analysis
損益分岐分析
break-even point
損益分岐点，収支分岐点
breakup
分解、分散、
解散

bridge loan
ブリッジローン、
つなぎ融資
brightness
輝度
broken lot
端株
broker
仲買人、ブローカー
brokerage
仲買、仲買業,
仲買手数料
brokerage allowance
仲介手数料割引
broker loan rate
証券担保貸付金利
browser
ブラウザ、閲覧ソフト
bucket shop
闇証券業者、
場外取引店
budget
予算、予算案
budget mortgage
バジェットモーゲージ
buffer stock
緩衝在庫
building code
建築基準法
building line
建築境界線
building loan agreement
建築融資契約
building permit
建築許可（証）
built-in stabilizer
内蔵スタビライザー
自動安定装置
bull
強気市場、強気筋
bulletin
告示する、掲示する
bulletin board system (BBS)
電子掲示板システム
bull market
強気相場、強気市場
bunching
集群、束、束ねること
bundle-of-rights theory
諸権利の束理論
burden of proof
挙証責任、立証責任
bureau
局、省
bureaucrat
官僚
burnout
ストレスによる肉体的・
精神的疲労
business
ビジネス、事業、
業務
business combination
企業合同、合併
business conditions
商況、景気
business cycle
景気循環
business day
営業日、平日

business ethics
ビジネス倫理、商業倫理
business etiquette
ビジネス・エチケット、
商売上の礼儀作法
business interruption
事業中断
business reply card
切手不用返信はがき、
商用返信はがき
business reply envelope
切手不用返信封筒、
商用返信封筒
business reply mail
商用［業務用］返信郵便物、
返信用郵便
business risk exclusion
事業リスク排除
business-to-business advertising
企業向け広告
bust-up acquisition
解体買収、破産買収
buy
買収する、購入する
buy-and-sell agreement
相互売買協定
buy-back agreement
買戻し約定
buy down
（頭金を多く払って買う）
バイダウン方式
buyer
買手、バイヤー
buyer behavior
購買行動
buyer's market
買手市場
buy in
処分買い、買戻し、
自己落札
buying on margin
思惑買い，信用買い
buy order
買注文
buyout
買収、買占め
buy-sell agreement
相互売買協定
buzz words
専門的な響きを持つ流行語、
もったいぶった専門用語
bylaws
(会社の）付随定款、規則、
内規、細則、付則
by-product
副産物、副製品
by the book
正確に、正式に、定石どお
りに

C

cable transfer
電信為替
cache
キャッシュ、貯蔵所、
貯蔵物
cadastre
土地台帳
cafeteria benefit plan
カフェテリアプラン（保険・退職年金などの）
calendar year
暦年
call
買付選択権、
コール(短期資金)
callable
請求次第支払われる、
(債権)償還請求できる
call feature
繰り上げ償還条項
call option
コール・オプション(コールは買付選択権、オプションは選択権付取引)
call premium
償還プレミアム
call price
買入価格、買入値段
call report
販売訪問報告書、
当局宛報告
cancel
解約する、取消す
cancellation clause
解除約款、解約条項
cancellation provision clause
解約規定約款、
解除規定条項
capacity
資格、能力、
容量
capital
資本、元金
capital account
資本的資金勘定、
資本(金)勘定
capital assets
固定資産、
資本資産
capital budget
資本予算
capital consumption allowance
資本(資産)減耗引当、
資本消耗引当金

capital contributed in excess of par value
額面価額超過分出資資本
capital expenditure
資本支出
capital formation
資本形成
capital gain (loss)
資本売却所得(損失)、
資本売却差益(差損)
capital goods
資本財
capital improvement
資本的支出とみられる改良、
設備改良
capital intensive
資本集中的
capital investment
設備投資、資本投資
capitalism
資本主義
capitalization rate
資本化率
capitalize
資本化する、
資本に組入れる
capitalized value
資本還元価値、
資本化価値
capital lease
資本リース契約
capital loss
資本売却差損
capital market
資本市場、
長期金融市場
capital nature flight
資本自然逃避
capital rationing
資本割当、資本制限、
資本不足
capital requirement
資金需要、
必要資本量
capital resource
資本資源
capital stock
資本金、資本株式、総株数
capital structure
資本構造、資本構成
capital surplus
資本余剰金
capital turnover
資本の回転、資本回転率
caps
上限、最高限度
capslock key
キャップスロックキー
captive finance company
専属金融会社
cargo
積荷、船荷、貨物
cargo insurance
積荷保険、貨物保険
carload rate
貸切扱運賃率
carrier
運送業者、運搬設備
carrot and stick
ニンジンと鞭、飴と鞭
carryback
貸越し分

carrying charge
保管費、諸掛、
前払経費
carryover
繰延、繰越(金)
cartage
(荷車)運賃、運搬費
cartel
連合企業、カルテル
case-study method
事例研究法
cash
現金、現金化する
cash acknowledgement
現金受領書、
現金受取証明書
cash basis
現金主義
cashbook
現金出納帳
cash budget
現金予算
cash buyer
現金購入者
cash cow
黒字部門、財源、
ドル箱部門、儲かる商品
優良株
cash disbursement
現金支払い、現金払い
cash discount
現金割引
cash dividend
現金配当
cash earnings
現金収入
cash equivalence
現金等価
cash flow
キャッシュ・フロー、
現金流出入
cashier
出納係
cashier's check
銀行小切手、
支払人小切手
cash market
現金市場
cash on delivery (COD)
貨物引換払い、
代金引替渡し
cash order
要求払為替手形、
現金支払票、現金注文
cash payment journal
現金支払帳
cash position
現金持ち高、資金繰り
cash ratio
現金比率、
現金準備(預金)率
cash register
金銭登録機、
キャッシュ・レジスター
cash reserve
現金準備、支払準備
cash surrender value
解約払戻金
casual laborer
日雇労働者、自由労働者
casualty insurance
災害保険

catastrophe hazard
大災害による危険
catastrophe policy
大災害保険証券
cats and dogs
がらくた株、
くだらぬ商品
cause of action
訴因、訴権
CD-writer/CD-burner
CD ライター／CD バーナー
cell definition
セルの定義
cell format
セルの形式
censure
非難(する)、不信任、
central bank
中央銀行
central business district (CBD)
商業中心地区
central buying
一括仕入れ
centralization
集権化、中央集権
central planning
集権的計画、中央計画
central processing unit (CPU)
中央処理装置、中央演算処理装置、CPU
central tendency
中心傾向
certificate of deposit (CD)
預金証書、有価証券預証
certificate of incorporation
会社設立許可証、法人設立許可証
certificate of occupancy
居住証明、建物使用許可証
certificate of title
権利証書
certificate of use
使用許可書
certification
証明、保証、証明書
certified check
支払保証小切手
certified finical statement
監査証明済み財務諸表
certified mail
受取証明郵便、書留郵便
C&F
運賃込み値段(条件)
chain of command
指揮系統、命令系統
chain feeding
連鎖的補給（供給)
chain store
チェーンストア
chairman of the board
取締役会長
chancery
衡平法裁判所、
エクイティ裁判所
change
変動、変更、換算、
両替賎、両替する
change of beneficiary provision
受益者条項の変更

channel of distribution
流通経路、ディストリビューション・チャンネル
channel of sales
販売経路
character
文字、キャラクター、字
charge
請求する、請求代金、
charge buyer
掛け買い客、信用取引客
chart
図、チャート、図表
charter
設立免許状、基本定款、用船契約(証券)、借上げ使用する(自動車など)
chartist
チャーティスト、
株式チャート作成・分析者
chart of accounts
勘定科目一覧表
chat forum
チャット広場、
チャットフォーラム
chattel
家財、動産
chattel mortgage
動産抵当、動産担保
chattel paper
動産抵当証券
check
小切手、
小切手を振出す
check digit
検査数字
check-kiting
空手形を振り出す、
手形詐欺
check protector
チェック・プロテクター
check register
チェック・レジスター、
小切手振出し記録簿
check stub
小切手の控え
chief executive officer
最高経営責任者
（会長である場合が多い）
chief financial officer
最高財務責任者
chief operating officer
最高（業務）執行責任者
（社長）
child and dependent care credit
児童・扶養家族養護控除
chi-square test
カイ二乗分布
churning
過度な売買勧誘、不当な回転商い
CIF
保険料運賃込み値段
cipher
暗号、
暗号文
circuit
巡回、迂回、
回路
circuit board
回路基板

civil law
民法
civil liability
市民的責任義務
civil penalty
民事刑罰
claim
請求(権)、
損害賠償を請求する
class
集合、集団
class action B shares
B株クラスアクション、
B株集団代表訴訟
classification
分類、各付け
classified stock
発行別分類株、
選別株
clause
条項
clean
きれいな、
間違いのない、
完全な
clean hands
潔白、汚れなき手の原則
cleanup fund
諸事整理資金、最終処理費基金
clear
清算する、皆済する、一掃する、見切売りする
clearance sale
残品見切販売、在庫一掃セール、クリアランスセール
clearinghouse
クリアリングハウス、手形交換所
clear title
無傷の権利
clerical error
記帳ミス、誤記
clerk
事務員、裁判所書記官
client
依頼人、クライアント
clipboard
クリップボード
close
非公開の、
限られた
close corporation plan
株式非公開会社方式、
閉鎖会社方式
closed account
締切済み勘定
closed economy
封鎖経済、
クローズドエコノミー
closed-end mortgage
閉鎖担保
（モーゲージ）
closed-end mutual fund
閉鎖型投資信託、
クローズドエンド型投資信託
closed stock
セット品
closely held corporation
閉鎖的所有会社
close out
閉鎖、店仕舞

closing
終結、取引終了
closing agreement
最終的合意
closing cost
不動産売買手数料
closing date
決算日、締切日

closing entry
決算記入、決算仕訳
closing inventory
期末棚卸(高)、
期末在庫
closing price or closing quote
終値、引値
closing statement
最終陳述、
最終報告書
cloud on title
権原の瑕疵、権原への疑義
cluster analysis
クラスター分析、
集団化分析
cluster housing
集合住宅，集合家屋
cluster sample
クラスターサンプル、
集落標本
cluster sampling
集落標本抽出
code
規則、慣例
code of ethics
倫理規範
codicil
遺言補足書、追加条項
coding of accounts
会計用語の符号化、
勘定符号法
coefficient of determination
決定係数
coinsurance
共同保険
cold canvass
飛び込み訪問
collapsible corporation
泡沫法人、泡沫会社
collateral
担保物件
collateral assignment
担保の譲渡
collateralize
担保として使う、
担保により保証する
collateralized mortgage obligation (CMO)
不動産抵当証書担保債券、
抵当付きモーゲージ証書
colleague
同僚、同業者
collectible
取り立てできる、
収集可能な、収集品
collection
徴収、集金、
収集物
collection ratio
代金回収率
collective bargaining
団体交渉

collusion
共謀、通謀、馴れ合い訴訟
collusive oligopoly
共謀寡占
column chart/graph
カラム図表／グラフ、
縦列図表／グラフ
combinations
組合わせ、連合体

comfort letter
コンフォートレター
（資金などの援助提供する旨の念書)
command
命令(する)、指揮(する)
command economy
指令経済
commencement of coverage
（保険契約）適用の開始
commercial
商業の、貿易の
commercial bank
商業銀行
commercial blanket bond
商業包括債券
commercial broker
商業ブローカー
commercial credit insurance
商業信用保険
commercial forgery policy
商業偽造保険
commercial forms
商業書式
commercial health insurance
商業健康保険
commercial law
商法
commercial loan
銀行貸付、商業融資
commercial paper
商業手形
commercial property
営業用不動産
commercial property policy
営利損害保険
commingling of funds
ファンドの合同運用
commission
手数料、コミッション
commission broker
仲買人
commitment
約束、公約、売買約定
commitment free
契約義務免責
commodities futures
商品先物取引き
commodity
商品、物品、必需品、
貨物
commodity cartel
商品カルテル
common area
共通範囲、共通域
common carrier
運送業者、運送会社、
公衆通信業者

common disaster clause or survivorship clause
共通災害条項、
生存者取得権条項、
同時災害条項
common elements
共通ブロック要素
common law
慣習法、判例法
common stock
通常株、普通株
common stock equivalent
普通株等価物、
準普通株式
common stock fund
普通株ファンド
common stock ratio
通常株率、普通株率
communications network
通信網、通信ネットワーク
communism
共産主義
community association
地域自治会
community property
夫婦共有財産
commutation right
金納化権、(生産物地代から貨幣地代への転化)、
(支払方法などの)振替
commuter
通勤者
commuter tax
通勤税
co-mortgagor
共同抵当権設定者
company
企業、会社
company benefits
会社給付(金)
company car
社用車
company union
御用組合、企業別組合
comparables
匹敵物、比較できる物
comparable worth
男女同一賃金原則
comparative financial statements
比較財務諸表
comparative negligence
過失相殺、比較過失
comparison shopping
競争品調査
compensating balance
相殺残金、補償預金
compensating error
相殺誤差
compensation
補償、賠償金、報酬、
compensatory stock options
補整的自社株購入権
compensatory time
代休
competent party
適格当事者
competition
競争
competitive bid
競争入札

competitive party
競争当事者
competitive party method
競争当事者方法
competitive strategy
競争戦略
competitor
競争相手、競争企業
compilation
編集、編纂、編纂著作物
compiler
編集者、コンパイラー（コンピューターの機械語翻訳プログラム）
compliant
申し立て、告訴状、訴状
complete audit
完全監査
completed contract method
完成契約方法
completed operations insurance
完成工事保険
completion bond
完成保証債券
complex trust
複合信託
compliance audit
準拠性監査、コンプライアンス監査
component part
構成要素、構成部分
composite depreciation
包括減価償却、
総合償却
composition
一部返済金、和解
compound growth rate
複合成長率
compound interest
複利
compound journal entry
複合仕訳記入
comprehensive annual financial report (CAFR)
総合年次財務報告書
comprehensive insurance
総合保険
compress
圧縮、短縮する
comptroller
財務部長、
会計検査官、監査官
compulsory arbitration
強制裁定、強制仲裁
compulsory insurance
強制保険
compulsory retirement
強制退職
computer
コンピューター、
電子計算機
computer-aided
コンピューターに補助された
concealment
隠蔽、隠匿、
告知義務違反
concentration banking
集中的預金

concept test
コンセプト・テスト
concern
利害関係、会社、企業
concession
譲与、特権、利権
conciliation
斡旋、調停
conciliator
調停者
condemnation
土地収用・接収・没収、有罪の判決
conditional contract
条件付契約
condition precedent
先行条件
conditional sale
条件付販売、条件付売約
conditional-use permit
条件付使用許可
condition subsequent
後行条件
conference call
会議通話
confidence game
（人の信頼につけこむ）
詐欺、信用詐欺
confidence interval
信頼区間
confidence level
信頼水準、信頼性のレベル
confidential
秘密の、機密の
confirmation
確定、確認
conflict of interest
利害の不一致、利害の衝突
conformed copy
正式な写し、合法の写し
confusion
混同、混乱
conglomerate
複合企業、
コングロマリット
conservatism, conservative
保守主義、保守的な
consideration
報酬、対価、約因
consignee
引受人、荷受人、受託者
consignment
委託、委託販売、委託貨物、委託販売品
consignment insurance
委託（品）保険
consignor
荷送人、委託者、
荷主
consistency
一貫性、無矛盾性
console
コンソール
consolidated financial statement
連結財務諸表
consolidated tax return
総合納税申告書
consolidation loan
総合ローン、合併融資、併合ローン

consolidator
コンソリデータ、混載業者、統合整理者
consortium
コンソーシアム、
共同事業体、配偶者権
constant
一定の、変わらない、定数
constant dollars
恒常ドル、不変ドル
constant-payment loan
等支払ローン
constituent company
構成会社
constraining (limiting) factor
制約要素
construction loan
建築ローン、建設融資
constructive notice
擬制悪意
constructive receipt of income
推定所得受領（学説）
consultant
コンサルタント、顧問、相談役
consumer
消費者
consumer behavior
消費者行動
consumer goods
消費財、消費物資
consumerism
消費者(優先)主義、
消費者運動
consumer price index (CPI)
消費者物価指数
consumer protection
消費者保護
consumer research
消費者調査
consumption function
消費関数
container ship
コンテナ船
contestable clause
問題条項、異議条項
contingency fund
臨時資金、危険準備金、
偶発損失積立金、
緊急用積立金
contingency planning
非常事態計画、
不測事態対応計画
contingency table
分割表
contingent fee
全面成功報酬
contingent liability
偶発債務、不確定責任
contingent liability (vicarious liability)
偶発債務
（代位責任）
continuing education
継続教育、生涯教育
continuity
継続性、連続性
continuous audit
継続監査

continuous process
連続工程
continuous production
連続生産
contra-asset account
資産控除科目、資産対照勘定
contract
契約、請負
contract carrier
契約輸送業者、契約輸送業
contraction
縮小、制限、短縮
contract of indemnity
損害填補契約
contractor
請負人、請負会社
contract price (tax)
契約価格(税)、
協定価格（税）
contract rate
契約運賃、契約料金
contract rent
契約家賃
contrarian
逆張り投資家、
人と逆の行動を取る人
contribution
寄付金、保険料
contribution profit, margin
貢献利益、貢献マージン
contributory negligence
寄与過失
contributory pension plan
拠出年金制
control
管理、支配
control account
統轄勘定、統制勘定
control key
コントロールキー、
Ctrl キー
controllable costs
管理可能費、管理内経費、
統制可能原価
controlled company
子会社、被支配会社
controlled economy
統制経済
controller
監査役、コントローラー、
会計検査官
controlling interest
経営支配権、
会社支配に十分な持ち株
convenience sampling
便宜標本法、簡易標本法
conventional mortgage
無保証抵当貸付け
conversion
換算、現金化、
転換
conversion cost
加工費
conversion factor for employee contributions
従業員拠出換算係数
conversion parity
転換平価
conversion price
切換価格、転換価格

conversion ratio
換算率(通貨の)、
転換比率
convertible term life insurance
転換可能定期生命保険
convey
運搬する、
（財産・権利を）
譲渡する
conveyance
運搬、譲渡
cooling-off period
冷却期間、
クーリングオフ期間
co-op
生活協同組合、
生活協同組合売店
cooperative
協同組合の、共同の、
協同組合
cooperative advertising
共同広告、協同広告
cooperative apartment
共同住宅マンション
copy-protected
コピー防止
（機能付き）の
copyright
版権、著作権
cornering the market
買い占め、市場独占
corporate bond
社債、法人債券
corporate campaign
企業キャンペーン
corporate equivalent yield
社債等価利回り
corporate strategic planning
企業戦略計画
corporate structure
企業構造、会社体質
corporate veil
企業ベール
corporation
企業、株式会社、法人
corporeal
物質的な、有形の
corpus
元金、元本、資本金
correction
修正、補正
correlation coefficient
相関係数
correspondent
通信者、取引先
corrupted
破損した、
原形が失われた
cosign
共同署名者
cost
原価、費用
cost accounting
原価会計、
原価計算
cost application
費用配分
cost approach
費用的アプローチ

cost basis
原価主義、原価基準
cost-benefit analysis
費用・便益分析
cost center
原価中心点、原価部門
cost containment
費用抑制
cost-effectiveness
費用有効度、費用効果
cost method
コスト主義、原価法
cost objective
費用目標
cost of capital
資本コスト
cost of carry
持越し費用
cost of goods manufactured
製造原価
cost of goods sold
売上原価、販売原価
cost-of-living adjustment (COLA)
生計費調節、
(賃金の)生活費調節
cost overrun
予算超過、（原価）
見積超過
cost-plus contract
利益加算契約、
原価加算契約
cost-push inflation
コストインフレ、
費用圧力インフレ
cost records
原価記録
co-tenancy
共同借地（借家）、不動産
共同保有
cottage industry
家内工業
counsel
弁護士、法律顧問、弁護団、
助言
counterclaim
反訴、反対要求
countercycical policy
逆景気循環政策、景気対策
counterfeit
偽造（の）、模造品
countermand
取消命令、反対命令（を出
す）、命令撤回（をする）、
(注文の)取り消し
counterroffer
カウンターオファー、
返し申込み、修正申込み
coupon bond
利札付債権、
利札付社債
court of record
記録裁判所
covariance
共分散、共変量
covenant
契約(書)、捺印証書による
契約
covenant not to compete
非競争約款

cover
保証金、補償範囲、保険をかける
covered option
担保オプション
cracker
クラッカー（コンピューターネットワークに不法侵入しデータの悪用やシステム破壊等をする者）
craft union
職種別組合、
職業別組合
crash
失敗、破産、崩壊
crash (computer)
故障、クラッシュする、機能が停止する
creative black book
創造的ブラックリスト
creative financing
工夫した金融、例外的なローン
credit
信用、貸方、債権
credit analyst
信用分析家
credit balance
貸方残高、預金尻
credit bureau
商業興信所、
信用調査機関
credit card
クレジットカード
creditor
債権者、貸主
credit order
掛け買い注文
credit rating
信用格付け、信用等級
credit requirements
資金需要、信用必要条件
credit risk
信用リスク
credit union
信用組合
creeping inflation
忍び寄るインフレ
critical path method (CPM)
臨界経路法
critical region
危険域、臨界領域
crop
(不必要な部分を)
切り取る、
トリミングする
cross
交叉、交差する
cross-footing
クロスフッティング
cross merchandising
クロスマーチャンダイジング、相互取引
cross purchase plan
相互買入れ制度
cross tabulation
組合せ分類、クロス集計
crowd
中間、グループ
crowding out
追し出し、締め出し

crown jewels
重要部門、目玉、
高採算部門
crown loan
クラウン貸付サービス
cum dividend, cum rights or cum warrant
配当付、権利付またはカムワラント
cumulative dividend
累加配当、累積配当
cumulative liability
重複責任
cumulative preferred stock
累積優先株、
累加的優先株
cumulative voting
累積投票
curable depreciation
回復可能な減価
currency futures
通貨先物
currency in circulation
流通通貨、通貨流通高
current
流通、流動
current asset
流動資産
current assumption whole life insurance
現行引受け終身保険
current cost
現行費用、現在の費用
current dollars
経常ドル
current liabilities
流動負債、当座負債、
current market value
現行市場価格(価額)
current ratio
流動比率
current value accounting
時価会計
current yield
現在収益、現在利回り
cursor
カーソル
curtailment in pension plan
年金制度の縮小
curtesy
鰥夫産、かん夫権
curtilage
住宅付属庭地、
宅地
custodial account
保管口座、保管勘定
custodian
管理人、保管人
custody
保管、管理、保護、
監護権
customer profile
顧客のプロフィール、
顧客情報
customer service
顧客サービス
customer service representative
顧客サービス担当者
customs
関税

customs court
関税裁判所
cutoff point
カットオフポイント、
決算日
cyberspace
サイバースペース、
サイバー空間、仮想空間
cycle billing
周期請求方式、
循環請求方式
cyclical demand
循環的需要
cyclical industry
循環産業
cyclical stock
循環株
cyclical unemployment
循環的失業、周期的失業
cyclic variation
循環的変動、循環変動

D

daily trading limit
一日取引限度
daisy chain
連鎖、一連の取引活動、見せ掛けの活況取引、デージーチェーン
damages
損害賠償金
data
データ、資料
database
データベース
database management
データベース管理
data collection
データ収集
data maintenance
データ保守
data processing insurance
データ処理保険
data retrieval
データ検索
data transmission
データ伝送
date of issue
振出日、発行日
date of record
権利確定期日、記録日
dating
日付記入
deadbeat
資産の無い人、一文無し
dead-end job
将来性の無い職
deadhead
能なし、役立たず者、やる気のない奴
deadline
締切日、最終期限、準備金限界線
dead stock
売残り品、不良在庫、死蔵品
dead time
不動時間、不感時間
dealer
商人、卸売業者
death benefit
死亡見舞金、死亡給付金
debasement
(貨幣の)価値低下、品質低下
debenture
社債、債権、債務証書
debit
借方
debit memorandum
貸方票、貸方メモ
debt
借金、負債、債務

debt coverage ratio
債務回収比率
debt instrument
債務証書
debtor
借主、債務者、負債者
debt retirement
債券償還
debt security
債務証券
debt service
債務元利未払金
debt-to-equity ratio
負債比率
debug
デバッグ、バグを取る
decentralization
分散（化）、分権（化）、地方分権
deceptive advertising
詐欺広告、誇大広告
deceptive packaging
詐欺包装
decision model
決定モデル
decision support system (DSS)
コンピュータによる意思決定支援システム
decision tree
決定樹
declaration
公表、申告
declaration of estimated tax
見積税申告
declaration of trust
信託宣言
declare
公表する、申告する
declining-balance method
定率法
decryption
暗号解読
dedicated line
専用回線、専用ライン
dedication
専用、献身
deductibility of employee contributions
従業員負担金控除性
deduction
控除、控除額
deductive reasoning
演繹法、演繹的推理・論証
deed
捺印証書、譲渡証書
deed of trust
信託証書
deed restriction
捺印証書による不動産の使用権制限
deep discount bond
大幅割引債券
de facto corporation
事実上の会社
defalcation
使い込み、金銭不当流用、横領
default
不履行、債務不履行、滞納

default (computer)
デフォルト、省略値（時）
default judgment
欠席裁判、欠席判決
defeasance
契約の無効化、
契約解除条件
defective
不完全な、不良品
defective title
瑕疵ある権限
defendant
被告（人）
defense of suit against insured
被保険者（物）訴訟の弁護
defensive securities
防衛的証券、
価格安定性の高い証券
deferred account
繰延勘定
deferred billing
繰延請求
deferred charge
据置失費、繰延費用
deferred compensation
繰延補償
deferred compensation plan
繰延補償制度
deferred contribution plan
繰延負担金制度
deferred credit
繰延貸方項目
deferred group annuity
据置グループ年金
deferred interest bond
据置利子債券
deferred maintenance
繰延維持費、据置保守
deferred-payment annuity
延払い年金
deferred payments
延払い、据置払い
deferred profit-sharing
据置利益分配型退職年金
deferred retirement
延期退職
deferred retirement credit
据置退職金支払猶予
deferred wage increase
据置昇給
deficiency
不足、不足額、欠損
deficiency judgment
不足金判決
deficiency letter
不備通知書
deficit
欠損(金)、赤字
deficit financing
赤字財政、
赤字財政策
deficit net worth
負の純資産
deficit spending
(財政による)超過支出、
赤字支出
defined-benefit pension plan
確定給付年金制度

defined contribution pension plan
定額負担年金制度
deflation
デフレ、通貨収縮
deflator
デフレータ-、
価格修正因子
defunct company
抹消会社
degression
下降、(税率の)逓減
deindustrialization
逆工業化、重工業退化、
産業の空洞化
delegate
代表、派遣委員
delete
削除、抹消、削除する
delete key (del)
削除キー、Del キー
delinquency
義務不履行、職務怠慢、滞納
delinquent
義務不履行の、職務怠慢の、
delisting
銘柄表から外すこと、上場廃止
delivery
引渡し、受渡し、交付
delivery date
引渡日、交付日、決済日
demand
需要、要求、督促
demand curve
需要曲線
demand deposit
要求支払預金、別段預金
demand loan
要求払貸付、コール貸付金
demand note
一覧払約束手形、
要求払約束手形
demand price
需要価格、付値
demand-pull inflation
需要インフレ
demand schedule
需要表
demarketing
需要を抑制するための宣伝活動、逆拡販運動
demised premises
譲渡家屋（土地）
demographics
実体的人口統計
demolition
取壊し、破棄
demonetization
廃貨、
本位貨幣資格喪失
demoralize
（秩序・機能を）乱す、混乱させる、士気をくじく
demurrage
滞船料、
貨車留置料
demurrer
異議、妨訴抗弁

denomination
(度量衡の)単位、(貨幣の)呼称
density
密度、比率
density zoning
密度区分
department
省、局、部門
dependent
扶養家族
dependent coverage
扶養家族補償
depletion
（資源などの）消耗・減少・枯渇、減耗償却(費)
deposit
銀行預金、保証金
deposit administration plan
預託管理制度、
預託管理方式
deposit in transit
未達預金
deposition
証言録取(書)
depositors forgery insurance
預金者文書偽造保険
depository trust company (DTC)
投資信託会社
depreciable life
減価償却期間
depreciable real estate
減価償却不動産
depreciate
減価見積りをする、減価償却を求める、価格を下げる、価値が下がる
depreciated cost
減価償却対象原価
depreciation
価値低減、減価償却
depreciation recapture
減価償却額再徴収
depreciation reserve
減価償却積立金・準備金
depression
不景気、不況
depth interview
深層テスト、
深層面接
deregulation
規制撤廃、規制緩和
derived demand
派生需要、間接需要
descent
下降、相続
description
記述、説明書
descriptive memorandum
説明的備忘録
descriptive statistics
記述統計学
desk
編集部、編集主任
desktop publishing
デスクトップパブリッシング
destination file (network)
宛先ファイル、
（宛先ネットワーク）

detail person
プロパー、
販売店支援担当者
devaluation
平価切下げ
developer
ディベロッパー、開発業者
development
開発、開発した地区(土地)
development stage enterprise
発展段階企業、
成長途上企業
devise
(不動産の)遺贈、
遺贈財産
dialup
ダイアルアップ、
電話回線接続
diagonal expansion
対角線的拡張
diary
日誌、日記
differential advantage
特異性による優位
differential analysis
微分分析
differentiation strategy
差別化戦略
digits deleted
削除された桁数
dilution
希釈（例：労働希釈）、
希釈化
（１株当りの利益などの）
diminishing-balance method
定率減価償却法
diplomacy
外交、駆引き
direct access
直接アクセス
direct-action advertising
直接行動広告
direct charge-off method
損失直接処理方式
direct cost
直接費
direct costing
直接原価計算
directed verdict
指示評決
direct financing lease
直接金融型リース
direct investment
直接投資
direct labor
直接労働
direct liability
直接債務、確定負債
direct marketing
直接販売、
直接マーケティング
direct material
直接材料
director
取締役、重役、理事
directorate
重役会、役員会、理事会、
管理職

direct overhead
直接間接費
direct-reduction mortgage
直接減価償却法
direct response advertising
直接反応広告
direct sales
直売
direct production
直産
disability benefit
廃疾給付、労働不能給付
disability buy-out insurance
廃疾買取保険
disability income insurance
廃疾所得補償保険、
就業不能時所得補償保険
disaffirm
～を破棄する、
～を拒否する
disbursement
支出、支出金、出費
discharge
免除、解除、解雇、履行、
免責
discharge in bankruptcy
破産の取消、
破産の免責
discharge in lien
担保権の取消、先取特権の
取消
disciplinary layoff
懲戒停職
disclaimer
拒否、放棄、否認、
放棄声明書、否認声明書
disclosure
開示、公開
discontinuance of plan
計画停止、計画中止
discontinued operation
廃止事業、廃止部門
discount
割引額、割引する
discount bond
割引債券
discount broker
手形割引仲買人、
手形割引ブローカー
discounted cash flow
割引キャッシュフロー
discounting the news
ニュース予想による株式価
格付け
discount points
ディスカウントポイント
discount rate
公定歩合、
手形割引歩合
discount window
割引窓口
discount yield
割引利回り
discovery
証拠開示手続き
discovery sampling
発見のための抽出法
discrepancy
食い違い、不一致
discretion
自由裁量、裁量権

discretionary cost
裁量原価
discretionary income
裁量所得
discretionary policy
裁量政策
discretionary spending power
裁量支出力
discrimination
差別、
差別待遇
diseconomies
不経済
dishonor
不渡り、支払拒絶、
引受拒否
disinflation
ディスインフレーション、
ディスインフレ政策
disintermediation
金融機関仲介離れ、
非仲介
disjoint events
ばらばらの出来事、
支離滅裂な出来事
disk
ディスク
disk drive
ディスクドライブ
dismissal
解雇、却下、放棄
dispatcher
発信人、発車係、発送者
disposable income
可処分所得
dispossess
(財産を)～から取り上げる、
奪う
dispossess proceedings
明渡し略式手続、
明渡し請求訴訟
dissolution
解散、解除
distressed property
差押不動産物件
distribution
分配、分布、流通
distribution allowance
流通引当金、
製造元による価格割引
distribution cost analysis
流通経費分析
distributor
小売業者、販売業者
diversification
多角経営、分散投資
diversified company
多角経営企業
divestiture
子会社の売却、投資の撤収、
企業分割
dividend
配当(金)、公債利息
dividend addition
追加配当
dividend exclusion
控除配当
dividend payout ratio
配当性向、配当支出割合
dividend reinvestment plan
配当再投資制度

dividend requirement
配当必要額
dividend rollover plan
配当借換え制度
dividends payable
未払配当金、
支払配当金
division of labor
分業
docking
ドッキング、結合
docking station
ドッキングステーション
documentary evidence
証拠書類、証書
documentation
文書添付、証拠書類提出
doing business as (DBA)
〜の名前で事業経営中
dollar cost averaging
定期定額買い、
ドルコスト平均法
dollar drain
ドル流出
dollar unit sampling (DUS)
ユニットドル価抽出
dollar value LIFO
ドル価先入先出法
domain name system
ドメイン名システム
domestic corporation
国内企業、国内法人
domicile
住所、手形支払場所
dominant tenement
要役地
donated stock
贈与株式
donated surplus
贈与剰余金
donor
贈与者、遺贈者
double click
ダブルクリック
double declining balance
倍額定率法、
二重漸減残高
double-digit inflation
二桁のインフレ
double-dipping
（年金と給料の）二重取り
double-entry accounting
複式簿記
double precision
倍精度
double taxation
二重課税
double time
倍額支給、賃金の倍額料金
double (treble) damages
倍額（3倍額）損害賠償
dower
寡婦産
download
ダウンロード、ダウンロードする
downpayment
頭金、手付金
downscale
規模を縮小する、
小型化する

downside risk
可能損失額
downstream
下流部門（の）
down tick
前回の引値より安い取引株価がつく相場の動き
downtime
非稼動時間、作業中止時間
downturn
(景気などの)下降、沈滞
downzoning
ゾーンを小さくする
dowry
結婚持参金
Dow theory
ダウ理論
draft
為替手形、支払指図書
draining reserves
準備金の枯渇・流出
draw
為替手形振出し
drawee
(為替手形の)支払人、(約束手形の)受取人
drawer
為替手形振出人
drawing account
引出金勘定
draw tool
描画ツール、画像作成ツール
drive
駆動、駆動装置、ドライブ
drop-down menu (pull-down menu)
ドロップダウンメニュー（プルダウンメニュー）
drop-shipping
生産者直送、製造元直送
dry goods
〔英〕穀類、〔米〕織物類
dual contract
二重契約
due bill
借用証書、有価証券引渡し書
due-on-sale clause
売却時返済条項
dummy
ダミー、模造品
dumping
ダンピング、不当廉売
dun
借金の催促をする、借金の督促
duplex copying (printing)
デュプレックスコピー（両面印刷）
duplication of benefits
重複手当
duress
強迫、強要

Dutch auction
競り下げ競売、逆競り

duty
任務、課税、(複数の場合)
関税

E

each way
手数料各自払い、
ブローカーの売買上の
early retirement
早期退職
early retirement benefits
早期退職手当
early withdrawal penalty
退職前引出罰則金
earned income
勤労所得、稼得所得
earnest money
手付金、保証金
earnings and profits
収益
earnings before taxes
税引前収益額、
税引前所得額
earnings per share
一株当り収益
earnings report
利益報告書
easement
地役権（土地の採光権や通行権など）
easy money
低金利の金、悪銭
econometrics
計量経済学
economic
経済の、経済学上の
economic analysis
経済分析
economic base
経済基盤、経済的基盤
economic depreciation
経済的減価
economic freedom
経済的自由
economic growth
経済成長
economic growth rate
経済成長率
economic indicators
経済指標
economic life
経済的耐用年数、
経済的寿命
economic loss
経済的損失
economic rent
経済地代、
(家主にとって)
採算の合う家賃
economics
経済学
economic sanctions
経済的制裁

economic system
経済体制
economic value
経済価値
economies of scale
規模の経済
economist
経済学者、
経済専門家
economy
経済機構、経済、節約
edit
編集、編集する
effective date
発効期日、有効日
effective debt
有効負債
effective net worth
有効純資産
effective rate
実効レート、実勢相場
effective tax rate
実効税率
efficiency
能率、効率、
有効性
efficient market
効率的市場
efficient portfolio
効率的ポートフォリオ
eject
取り出す、イジェクトする、
追い出す、立ち退かせる
ejectment
妨害排除訴訟、不動産占有
回復訴訟
elasticity of supply and demand
需要と供給の弾力性
elect
当選した、選ぶ、決める、
選挙する
electronic mail (email)
電子メール（Eメール）
eligibility requirements
資格要件
eligible paper
適格手形
email address
電子メールアドレス
emancipation
（束縛・因習・
身分制度からの）解放
embargo
輸出禁止、通商禁止
embed
埋め込む、組み込む、
はめ込む
embezzlement
使いこみ、横領
emblement
勤労果実、
作物収得権、人工耕作物
eminent domain
収用権
employee
従業員、雇い人、使用人
employee association
従業員組合
employee benefits
被用者給付、
従業員福利

employee contributions
従業員負担金
employee profit sharing
従業員利益共有制度
employee stock option
従業員自社株購入制度
employee stock ownership plan (ESOP)
従業員持株制度、従業員株式所有制度
employer
事業主、雇主、雇用者
employer interference
雇用者介入
employment agency
職業紹介所、職業安定所
employment contract
雇用契約
enable
可能にする、使用可能にする
enabling clause
権限賦与条項、授権条項
encoding
コード化
encroach
侵入する、侵害する
encroachment
権利の不法拡張、侵略、侵害、不法侵入
encryption
暗号化、コード化
encumbrance
（財産上の）負担、債務（抵当権など）
end of month
月末
endorsement or indorsement
裏書、保証
endowment
基金の寄付行為、寄贈、遺贈、養老資金、基本財産
end user
エンドユーザー、最終利用者
energy tax credit
エネルギー税控除
enjoin
命じる、差し止める、禁止する
enterprise
企業、事業
enterprise zone
企業地域、企業地区
entity
企業、実在物
entrepreneur
企業家、実業家
entry-level job
新米の仕事、初歩的な仕事入社段階の仕事
environmental impact statement (EIS)
環境影響報告書
EOM dating
EOM 日付、月末日付
equalization board
査定平準局

equal opportunity employer
機会均等主義雇用主
equal protection of the laws
法律の均等保護
equilibrium
均衡、平衡
equilibrium price
均衡価格
equilibrium quantity
均衡量
equipment
備品、設備、施設、装置
equipment leasing
設備・備品リース
equipment trust bond
設備信託債券
equitable
公平な、公正な、衡平法の
equitable distribution
公平な分配
equity
株式，財産物件の純粋価格、純資産価値
equity financing
持分金融（新株発行を伴う企業の資金調達のこと）
equity method
持分法
equity of redemption
衡平法上の受戻権
equity REIT
不動産投資信託
equivalent taxable yield
課税対象等価利回り
erase
消去する、消去
error
過失、誤差、エラー
error message
エラー・メッセージ
escalator clause
エスカレーター条項、均等変動条項
escape key (esc)
エスケープキー、Esc キー
escheat
復帰財産、
復帰によって没収する
escrow
条件付捺印証書、
第三者寄託（財産）、エスクロウ
escrow agent
条件付捺印証書受託者
espionage
スパイ行為、諜報活動
essential industry
基幹産業
estate
不動産(権)、財産(権)
estate in reversion
復帰不動産権
estate in severalty
単独保有財産権（資産）
estate planning
資産計画
estate tax
相続税、遺産税
estimate
予測する、見積（書）

estimated tax
見積税
estimator
見積人、推定量・
値
estoppel
禁反言
estoppel certificate
禁反言証書
estovers
必要物（離婚扶助料など）、
必要物収取権
ethical, ethics
道徳上の、倫理上の、
道徳、倫理
euro
ユーロ（通貨単位）
European Common Market
欧州共同市場
European Economic Community (EEC)
欧州経済共同体
eviction
追い立て、立ち退き
eviction, actual
現実の追い立て
eviction, constructive
擬制の追い立て
eviction, partial
部分的追い立て
evidence of title
権利書
exact interest
完全利子、完全利息、
正確な金利
"except for" opinion
監査人による監査不可意見
(書)
excess profits tax
超過利得税、超過利潤税
excess reserves
(銀行の)過剰準備、
過剰準備金
exchange
為替、取引所
exchange control
為替管理
exchange rate
為替相場、為替レート
excise tax
物品税、国内消費税
exclusion
除外、免責、控除金額
exculpatory
弁明の無罪を証明する
ex-dividend date
配当落ち期日
execute
履行する、実行する、執行
する、作成する
executed
履行された、
実行された
executed contract
履行契約
execution
執行、実行、
強制執行
executive
幹部役員、
行政部

executive committee
実行委員会、
執行委員会
executive perquisites
役員の役得、
役員への優遇措置
executor
遺言執行者
executory
行政上の、未履行の
exemption
免除、免税、
適用免除
exempt securities
免除証券
exercise
行使、用いる
exit interview
出口インタビュー
ex-legal
不法の、不法行為上の、
非合法な
expandable
拡張可能な
expansion
拡大、発展
expected value
期待値
expense
費用、支払
expense account
経費勘定
expense budget
経費予算
expense ratio
管理費率、経費率
expense report
経費報告書
experience refund
経験料率法による保険料金の返済
experience rating
経験料率法
expiration
満了、満期、期間経過
expiration notice
満期通知、
有効期間終了通知
exploitation
搾取、不法利用
exponential smoothing
指数平滑法
export
輸出、輸出する
Export-Import Bank (EXIMBANK)
輸出入銀行
exposure
摘発、曝露、エクスポージャー（融資者や投資者のリスクに曝される程度）
exposure draft
公開草案
express
特別の、
急行(便)の
express authority
明示的権限
express contract
明示的契約
extended coverage
拡張担保

extended coverage endorsement
拡張担保裏書き
extension
延長、延期
extension of time for filing
提出期限延長
extenuating circumstances
酌量すべき事情、軽減事由
external audit
外部監査
external documents
外部資料
external funds
外部資金
external report
社外報告（書）、外部の報告
extractive industry
採掘産業
extra dividend
特別配当
extraordinary dividends
臨時配当
extraordinary item
臨時項目
extrapolation
外挿法、補外法

F

fabricator
組立製造業者、加工業者
face amount
額面、額面価額
face interest rate
額面金利
face value
額面価額、表面価値
facility
施設、設備
facsimile
複写、ファックス
factor analysis
因子分析、要因分析
factorial
階乗の、問屋の、
階乗
factoring
売掛債権買取
factory overhead
製造間接費、
工場諸経費
fail to deliver
引渡不履行
fail to receive
引取不履行
failure analysis
不良分析
fair market rent
公正市場賃貸料
fair market value
公正市場価格
fair rate of return
適性収益率
fair trade
公正取引、互恵貿易
fallback option
最低補償オプション
fallen building clause
倒壊建物約款
false advertising
虚偽広告、不良広告
family income policy
家族所得保険
family life cycle
家族生活周期、家族のライフサイクル
family of funds
資金群、資金グループ
FAQ (frequently asked questions)
よく出される質問と、
それに対する回答をまとめたファイル、FAQ
farm surplus
余剰農産物、農産物余剰
fascism
ファシズム
fatal error
致命的誤り

favorable trade balance
貿易収支の黒字、
輸出超過
featherbedding
水増雇用
federal deficit
財政赤字、国家赤字
Federal Deposit Insurance Corporation (FDIC)
連邦預金保険会社
federal funds
(連邦準備銀行の)準備金
federal funds rate
準備金利率
Federal Reserve Bank
連邦準備銀行
Federal Reserve Board (FRB)
連邦準備制度理事会
Federal Reserve System (FED)
連邦準備制度
Federal Savings and Loan Association
連邦貯蓄貸付協会
Fed wire
連邦準備銀行間通信システム
fee
報酬、手数料、料金（入会金など）、相続不動産権
feeder lines
分配線、支線
fee simple or fee simple absolute
無条件相続不動産権、
単純不動産権
FHA mortgage loan
連邦住宅局住宅ローン
fidelity bond
身元保証保険、信用保険
fiduciary
受託者（の）、被信託者（の）、信託された
fiduciary bond
受託者保証書
field staff
現地スタッフ、
現場スタッフ
field theory of motivation
人間動機付け現場理論
file
書類とじ、提出する
file backup
ファイルバックアップ
file extension
ファイル拡張子
file format
ファイル形式
file transfer protocol (FTP)
ファイル転送プロトコル
fill or kill (FOK)
即時実行注文
final assembly
最終組立
finance charge
融資手数料、金融費用
finance company
金融会社
financial accounting
財務会計
financial advertising
金融広告

financial future
金融先物
financial institution
金融機関
financial intermediary
信用仲介機関、
金融仲介機関
financial lease
ファイナンスリース、
金融リース
financial management rate of return (FMRR)
財務管理収益率、
財テク収益率
financial market
金融市場、金融筋
financial position
金融状態、財政状態
financial pyramid
金融ピラミッド
financial statement
財務諸表
financial structure
金融組織、財務構造
financial supermarket
金融スーパーマーケット
financing
融資、資金調達
finder's fee
仲介手数料
finished goods
加工品、完成品
fire insurance
火災保険
firm
会社、企業、商社
firm commitment
真剣にかかわり合うこと、
確定約束
firm offer
回答期限付売買申し込み、
確定的申し込み、
確定価格提示
firm order
期限指定注文、確定注文
firm quote
確約値段
first in, first out (FIFO)
先入先出法
first lien
第1順位の留置権・先取権
first-line management
最優秀の経営、
第一線の経営
first mortgage
第一抵当
first-year depreciation
初年度減価償却
fiscal
国庫の、財政の、会計の
fiscal agent
財務代理人、
財務代理機関
fiscalist
フィスカリスト、
財政主義者
fiscal policy
財政政策
fixation
固定、定着、執着
fixed annuity
定額型年金

fixed asset
固定資産
fixed benefits
固定給付
fixed charge
確定負債、固定担保
fixed-charge coverage
固定担保補償(範囲)
fixed cost
固定原価、固定費用
fixed fee
固定料金
fixed income
固定収入、定額所得
fixed income statement
固定所得計算書
fixed-point number
固定少数点数
fixed premium
固定保険料
fixed-price contract
固定価格契約
fixed-rate loan
固定金利融資
fixture
備品
flanker brand
いんちきブランド、
いんちき商標
flash memory
フラッシュメモリー
flat
(市場が)不振の、均一な
flat rate
均一料金、定率
flat scale
定率
flat tax
一律課税、均等税
flexible budget
弾力性予算、変動予算
flexible-payment mortgage (FPM)
弾性支払住宅ローン
変動支払住宅ローン
flextime
フレックスタイム、
伸縮的労働時間
flight to quality
（危険投資から）安全投資への資金の流れ
float
変動、変動相場制、浮動証券、起債する
floater(会社設立の)発起人、包括保険、浮動証券
floating debt
一時借入金、流動負債、変動負債
floating currency exchange rate
浮動通貨交換レート
floating exchange rate
浮動為替相場(レート)
floating-point number
浮動小数点数
floating-rate note
変動金利手形、
変動利付債
floating securities
浮動証券

floating supply
短期在庫品、短期供給品
flood insurance
洪水保険
floor loan
最低融資
floor plan
間取図、床配置図、見取り図、平面図
floor plan insurance
担保商品保険、ディスプレイ用保険
flotation (floatation) cost
証券発行費用、設立費用
flowchart
フローチャート、生産工程一覧表、業務運行表
flow of funds
資金循環
fluctuation
変動、騰落
fluctuation limit
変動限界
flush (left/right)
左寄せ・左揃え、右寄せ・右揃え
follow-up letter
追いかけ状、続報
font
フォント、字体
footing
立場、入会金、合計（額）
footnote
脚注
forced page break
強制的ページ区切り
forced sale
公売、強制売却
forced saving
強制貯蓄
forecasting
予測、予想
foreclosure
抵当流れ、請戻権喪失
foreign corporation
外国企業
foreign direct investment 直接国外投資
foreign exchange
外国為替、外国為替取引
foreign income
外国所得
foreign investment
国外投資、海外投資
foreign trade zone
外国貿易地帯
forfeiture
(財産の)没収、失権、（契約の）失効
forgery
偽造、文書偽造、贋造、捏造、改竄、偽造物
format
フォーマット、書式、形式
formula investing
フォーミュラ投資方法
fortuitous loss
偶然損失、偶発的損失

forward
先物の、前方の、先の、送る、発送する
forward contract
先物契約、先渡し契約
forwarding company
運送業者
forward integration
製品・サービスの拡張(統合)、前向きの統合
forward pricing
先物価格付け
forward stock
先物株式
for you information (FYI)
ご参考のため
foul bill of landing
故障付き船荷証券
401(k) plan
米国の企業年金制度
fourth market
第四市場
fractional share
端株
frame rate
フレームレート、フレーム率、画面書換速度
franchise
営業特権、一手販売権、フランチャイズ
franchise tax
免許税、特許税
frank
率直な、無料配達郵便物
fraud
詐欺、不正行為
fraudulent misrepresentation
詐欺的不実表示
free alongside ship (FAS)
船側渡し
free and clear
(不動産が)抵当に入っていない、
留置権がつけられていない
free and open market
自由開放市場
free enterprise
自由企業、自由企業体制
freehold (estate)
自由保有権、
自由保有不動産
free market
自由市場、実勢市場
free on board (FOB)
本船渡し
free port
自由港
freight insurance
運賃保険
frequency
頻度、度数
frictional unemployment
摩擦的失業
friendly suit
友誼的訴訟

frontage
（建物・地所の）正面（幅）、向き、臨界地、隣接地
front-end load
先取り手数料、
当初販売手数料
front foot
間口幅
front money
仲買人への前払い金、
前貸し金
front office
本部、総務室
frozen account
凍結勘定
***F* statistic**
*F*ー統計
fulfillment
履行、実現
full coverage
完全適用範囲
full disclosure
完全開示
full faith and credit
全面的信用と信頼
full screen display
全画面表示、
全画面ディスプレイ
full-service broker
完全サービス提供ブローカー
fully diluted earnings per (common) share
(普通株)
1株当たり完全稀釈収益
fully paid policy
全額払込保険
functional authority
職能権限
functional currency
機能通貨
functional obsolescence
機能的陳腐化
functional organization
職能組織、機能組織
function key
機能キー、
ファンクションキー
fund accounting
資金会計
fundamental analysis
基礎分析
funded debt
長期借入金、長期債務
funded pension plan
長期年金制
funding
長期公債投資、
基金繰り入れ、
資金操作
fund-raising
資金調達
furlough
賜暇、休暇
future interest
将来権
futures contract
先物取引(契約)
futures market
先物市場

G

gain
所得、利益
gain contingency
利益の偶発性
galloping inflation
急進のインフレ
game card
ゲームカード
gaming
賭博、ギャンブル、賭け
gap
ギャップ、ずれ、格差、欠陥、間隙
gap loan
ギャップローン
garnish
差押える
garnishee
第三債務者
garnishment
債権差押え、差押え通知
gender analysis
性別分析
general contractor
一般請負人
general equilibrium analysis
一般均衡分析
general expense
一般営業費、一般経費
general fund
一般資金、一般財源
generalist
一般職、ゼネラリスト
general journal
一般仕訳帳
general ledger
総勘定元帳、一般元帳
general liability insurance
総合賠償責任保険
general lien
(不動産を除く)すべての物品に対する先取り特権
generally accepted accounting principles
一般に受け入れられている会計原則
general obligation bond
一般財源債、一般公債
general partner
無限責任社員、一般社員
general revenue sharing
一般交付金、
一般目的財務補助制度
general scheme
一般的構想
general strike
ゼネスト、
総同盟罷業

general warranty deed
無債権土地譲渡証書、
全般的瑕疵担保証書
generation-skipping transfer
世代を飛び越えた譲渡
generic appeal
(一般的な商品としての魅力)
generic bond
一般債券
generic market
一般市場
gentrification
(スラムなどの) 高級化
geodemography
地球人口統計学
gift
贈与
gift deed
贈与証書
gift tax
贈与税
girth
周囲の寸法、太さ、胴回り
glamor stock
花形株、投資家魅了株
glut
過多、供給過剰、過剰生産
goal
目標、目的
goal congruence
目標一致
goal programming
目標の計画
goal setting
目標設定
go-between
仲介者、媒介者
going long
見込み買い、思惑買い
going private
株式非公開化
going public
株式公開化
going short
思惑売り
goldbrick
見かけ倒しの、にせ物
goldbug
金本位制支持者、
黄金狂
golden handcuffs
黄金の手錠（転職防止のための給料上の特別優遇措置のこと)
golden handshake
（定年前の退職者に支払う）特別報酬、割増退職金
golden parachute
ゴールデンパラシュート（経営者の高額退職金を受ける旨の雇用契約)
gold fixing
金(きん)の建値決定、（ロンドン金市場の）金価格、
gold mutual fund
金鉱採掘会社投資信託
gold standard
金本位制

good delivery
適法受渡し、適格受渡し
証券の合格調達
good faith
誠実、誠意、善意
good-faith deposit
手付金
good money
高賃金、良貨
goodness-of-fit test
適合度検定
goods
財貨、商品
goods and services
物品とサービス
good-till-canceled order (gtc)
取消しまで有効な注文
good title
無傷の権利、良権原
goodwill
のれん、(店の)株、
営業権
grace period
(払込)猶予期間
graduated lease
賃貸料累進型リース
graduated payment mortgage (GPM)
累進返済方式抵当
graduated wage
累進式賃金
graft
不正利得、汚職（事件）、
収賄（事件）
grandfather clause
祖父条項、グランド
ファーザー条項
grant
補助（金）、交付（金）、
譲与
grantee
譲受人、被譲与者
grantor
譲与者
grantor trust
贈与信託
graph
図、図表、グラフ
graphics card
グラフィックスカード、図
形カード
gratis
無料で
gratuitous
無料の、無償の
gratuity
祝儀、チップ
graveyard market
墓場市場、活気のない市場
graveyard shift
深夜勤務、第三次作業
gray scale
グレイスケール、
無彩色スケール
great depression
大恐慌
greenmail
グリーンメール、
株式買い戻し工作

gross
全体の、総額の
gross amount
総額
gross billing
総額請求
gross earnings
総収益、総収入
gross estate
総財産、総不動産、総遺産
gross income
総所得、総収入
gross leasable area
総賃貸契約地域
gross lease
費用貸主持ちの賃貸借契約
gross national debt
国債総額
gross national expenditure
国民総支出
gross national product (GNP)
国民総生産
gross profit
総利益、総利潤
gross profit method
総益法
gross profit ratio
粗利益率、粗利潤率
gross rating point (GRP)
総視聴率
gross rent multiplier (GRM)
総賃貸料乗数
gross revenue
総収入、総収益
gross ton
英トン（２２４０ポンド）
gross weight
総重量、風袋込み重量
ground lease
土地賃貸し、
土地賃貸借
ground rent
(英)地代、借地料
group credit insurance
団体信用保険
group disability insurance
団体廃疾保険
group health insurance
団体健康保険
group life insurance
団体生命保険
growing-equity mortgage (FEM)
持分成長担保
growth fund
成長型投資信託ファンド
growth rate
成長率、増加率
growth stock
成長株式
guarantee
保証、担保（物件）、被保証人、保証する
guaranteed annual wage (GAW)
保証年間賃金
guaranteed bond
(元金利子支払などの)
保証債券、保証付債券
guaranteed income contract (GIC)
所得保証契約
guaranteed insurability
保証被保険性

guaranteed mortgage
保証担保
guaranteed security
保証証券
guaranteed letter
保証レター
guarantee of signature
署名保証
guarantor
保証人、引受人
guaranty
保証契約、保証行為、担保
guardian
後見人、保護者、監視者
guardian deed
後見人捺印証書
guild
ギルド、同業組合

H

habendum
物権表示条項
hacker
ハッカー、
コンピュータへの不法侵入者
half duplex
半二重（伝送方式）
half-life
半減期
halo effect
ハロー効果、後光
（背光）効果
hammering the market
マーケットの売りたたき
handling allowance
取扱い準備金、取扱い費
hangout
溜まり場、低級娯楽場所
hard cash
正金、硬貨
hard currency
硬貨、交換可能通貨、
ハードカレンシー
hard disk
ハードディスク
hard dollars
実際の現金による支払
hard drive
ハードドライブ
hard goods
耐久財、ハードグッヅ
hard money
硬貨、現金
hard return
ハードリターン
hardware
ハードウェア
hardwired
ハードワイヤード、
配線による
hash total
ハッシュ合計、検査和
hatch
ハッチ
exclusion of coverage
保護適用除外
hazard insurance
危険保険
head and shoulders
ヘッドアンド
ショルダー、三山天井、
三尊
headhunter
人材スカウト会社
(の社員）、ヘッドハンター
（会社）、人材引き抜き係
head of household
世帯主

header
見出し、ヘッダー、
見出し部
health maintenance organization (HMO)
健康維持機構
hearing
聴取会、審問、聴覚、
heavy industry
重工業
hectare
ヘクタール
hedge
売り（買い）つなぎ、
両掛け
heirs
相続人、法定相続人、
継承者
heirs and assigns
相続人ならびに譲受人
help index
ヘルプ索引
help screen
ヘルプ画面、ヘルプ
スクリーン
help wizard
ヘルプウィザード
heterogeneous
異質の
heuristic
ヒューリスティック、
発見にやくだつ、発見的
hidden agenda
隠れた処理事項
hidden asset
含み資産
hidden inflation
隠れたインフレ、
隠されたインフレ
hidden tax
隠れた税金
hierarchy
ヒエラルキー、階級制度
high credit
高い信用、
ハイクレジット
highest and best use
最高最善の使用
（用途）
high flyer
高値株、ハイフライヤー
high-grade bond
優良証券、優良債券
high-involvement model
係わりの高いモデル
highlight
強調表示、強調表示する
high resolution
高解像度、
高レゾリューション
highs
高値
high-speed
高速度
high technology
ハイテク、高度技術、
高度先端技術
high-tech stock
ハイテク株
historical cost
実際原価、
歴史的原価

historical yield
歴史的歩留、歴史的生産高
historical structure
歴史的構造物、歴史的組織
hit list
対象物リスト、人気リスト、ヒットリスト
hit the bricks
ストライキをする
hobby loss
ホビーロス、趣味（道楽）による損失条項
holdback
停止遅延、阻止、保留物
holdback pay
支払保留賃金
holder in due course
正当所持人
holder of record
記録保持者
hold-harmless agreements
賠償責任免除特約
hold harmless clause
賠償責任免除条項
holding
支持、保有、所有
holding company
親会社、持ち株会社
holding fee
保有手数料
holding period
保有期間
holdover tenant
保有期間満了後占有者
home key
ホームキー
homeowner's association
住宅所有者協会
homeowner's equity account
住宅所有者持分勘定
homeowner's policy
住宅所有者保険証券(または約款)
homeowner warranty program (HOW)
住宅所有者保証プログラム
home page
ホームページ
homestead
家屋敷
homestead tax exemption
不動産税免除
homogeneous
同質的な、均質的な
homogeneous oligopoly
同質的寡占
honor
引き受けて支払う,
引き受ける、支払う
honorarium
謝礼金
horizontal analysis
水平分析
horizontal channel integration
水平チャンネル統合
horizontal combination
水平結合
horizontal expansion
水平拡張

horizontal merger
水平合併
horizontal specialization
水平特殊化
horizontal union
水平合併、水平団結
hot cargo
盗品貨物、密輸貨物、
ホットカーゴ
hot issue
人気新銘柄、緊急問題、
注目材料
hot stock
高人気の新規発売株
house
家屋、住宅
house account
社内勘定
house to house
戸ごとの、家から家へ
house-to-house sampling
家をまわって抽出見本をとる
huse-to-house selling
家をまわって販売
housing bond
住宅証券、
住宅債券
housing code
住宅基準法規
housing starts
住宅着工件数
huckster
行商人、宣伝屋、
強引なセールスマン
human factors
人的要素、人的要因
human relations
人的関係論、ヒューマン
リレーションズ
human resource accounting
人的資源会計
human resources
人的資源
human resources management (HRM)
人的資源管理
hurdle rate
投資の期待率収益
hush money
口止め料
hybrid annuity
混合型確定年金、
複合確定年金
hyperinflation
超インフレーション、
ハイパーインフレーション
hypertext
ハイパーテキスト
hypothecate
（不動産等を）
担保にいれる
hypothesis
仮定、仮説、前提
hypothesis testing
仮説テスト

I

icon
アイコン
ideal capacity
理想能力、収容力
idle capacity
遊休能力
illegal dividend
不法配当
illiquid
非流動的、
流動資産に欠けている
image
画像、像、イメージ
image advertising
イメージ広告
image definition
画像定義
image file
画像ファイル
impacted area
インパクトエリア、
衝撃を受ける地域または範囲
impaired capital
減殺資本
impasse
袋小路、難局、
窮境
imperfect market
不完全市場
imperialism
帝国主義
implied
含蓄された、言外の
implied contract
黙示的契約
implied easement
黙示的地役権
implied in fact contract
黙示的実際契約
implied warranty
黙示的保証
import
輸入
import quota
輸入割当
imposition
賦課、課税, 負担
impound
押収する、没収する
impound account
口座を押収する
imprest fund, imprest system
定額前渡し資金、定額（資金）前渡し制
improved land
改良された土地
improvement
改良、増進

improvements and betterments insurance
改良設備保険

imputed cost
帰属原価

imputed income
帰属所得

imputed interest
帰属利子

imputed value or imputed income
帰属価値または帰属所得

inactive stock or inactive bond
不活発株、不人気株、
または不人気債券

inadvertently
不注意に

incapacity
無能、無力、
無能力

incentive fee
奨励報酬

incentive pay
報酬金、奨励金

incentive wage plan
奨励賃金制、奨励金計画

incentive stock option (ISO)
自社株奨励購入権

inchoate
未終結の

incidental damages
偶発損害賠償金

income
所得、収益

income accounts
収入勘定、所得勘定

income approach
所得接近方

income averaging
所得平均化

income bond
収益債券、収益社債

income effect
所得効果

income group
所得階層、所得層

income in respect of a decedent
死亡者に係わる所得

income property
利益財産、収益財産

income redistribution
所得再分配

income replacement
代替所得

income splitting
所得分割法

income statement
所得計算書、
損益計算書

income stream
所得流れ

income tax
所得税

income tax return
所得税申告、
所得税申告書

incompatible
互換性がない

incompetent
無能力な、証言能力のない、禁治産者
incontestable clause
不可争条項
inconvertible money
不兌換貨幣
incorporate
法人を設立する、組み込む
incorporation
合併、会社設立、会社
incorporeal property
無体財産
incremental analysis
増分分析
incremental cash flow
増分キャッシュフロー
incremental spending
増分支出
incurable depreciation
矯正不能減価償却
indemnify
補償する、弁償する
indemnity
損害賠償、弁償金
indent
インデント、字下げすること
indenture
契約書、証書
independence
独立、自立
independent adjuster
独立調停人、独立損害査定人
independent contractor
請負人、独立契約者
independent store
独立店舗
independent union
独立労働組合、単独組合
independent variables
独立変数、自変数
indeterminate premium life insurance
不確定保険料生命保険
index
指数、目録、索引
indexation
インデックス化、指数化
index basis
指数基準
indexed life insurance
指数化された生命保険
indexed loan
指数化された貸付金、指数化された融資
index fund
物価指数資金
indexing
インデクシング
index lease
インデックスリース
index options
株価指数オプション
indirect cost
間接費
indirect labor
間接労働

indirect overhead
間接諸経費
indirect production
間接生産
individual bargaining
個別交渉、個人交渉
individual life insurance
個人生命保険
individual retirement account (IRA)
個人退職積立勘定
inductive reasoning
帰納的推理
industrial
産業の、工業の、工業用の
industrial advertising
産業広告
industrial consumer
産業消費者、工業消費者
industrial engineer
産業（または工業）技師、産業（または工業）エンジニア
industrial fatigue
産業的疲労
industrial goods
生産財、工業生品
industrialist
産業経営者、実業家、工業家
industrial park
工業団地
industrial production
工業生産、工業生産額
industrial property
工業所有権
industrial psychology
産業心理学
industrial relations
労使関係
industrial revolution
産業革命
industrial union
産業別組合、産業別労働組合
industry
産業、工業
industry standard
産業基準
inefficiency in the market
市場における非能率（低能率）
infant industry agreement
幼稚産業合意
inferential statistics
推論的統計、推測的統計
inferior goods
劣等財、低級財、下級品
inferred authority
推測された権威
inflation
インフレ
inflation accounting
インフレ会計
inflationary gap
インフレギャップ
inflationary spiral
螺旋状の物価上昇
inflation endorsement
（物保険の）インフレ裏書（条項）

inflation rate
インフレ率
informal leader
インフォーマルリーダー、非公式リーダー
information flow
情報の流れ
information page
インフォーメーションョン呼び出し
information return
支払調書
infrastructure
下部構造、下部組織、経済基盤
infringement
権利侵害、法規違反
ingress and egress
土地家屋への出入り、家屋出入り権
inherent explosion clause
(物保険の)特定立地(工場などの)爆発危険条項
inherit
相続する
inheritance
物的財産（法定）相続、法定不動産相続
inheritance tax
遺産相続税、遺産取得税、相続税
in-house
社内の
initial public offering (IPO)
新規株式公募
initiative
率先の、率先、発議権
injunction
強制命令、差止め命令、禁止命令
injunction bond
差止命令債務証書
injury independent of all other means
全ての他の手段から独立した権利侵害
inland carrier
内地運送業者
inner city
都会の中の中心市街地、大都会の既成市街地
innovation
新規軸、革新、技術革新
in perpetuity
永久に、終期の定めなく
inside information
内部情報
inside lot
中敷地
insider
インサイダー、内部者
insolvency
債務超過、支払不能、破産
insolvency clause
債務超過条項
inspection
審査、検査、点検

input
入力
input field
入力フィールド
input mask
入力フィールド
input-output device
入出力装置
installation
インストレーション、導入、設置
installment
割賦払い、割賦払金、月賦
installment contract
賦払契約
installment sale
月賦販売、割賦売上
institutional investor
機関投資家
institutional lender
機関貸手
instrument
証書、証券、手段
instrumentalities of transportation
移動（輸送）方法、手段
instrumentality
道具、手段
insurability
保険適合性
insurable interest
被保険利益
insurable title
保険可能権原、権利証書
insurance
保険、保険契約
insurance company (insurer)
保険会社（保険者）
insurance contract
保険契約、保険契約書
insurance coverage
保険担保
insurance settlement
保険金解決、保険金決済
insured
被保険者、保険契約者
insured account
保険金額
insurgent
反者、暴徒、造反分子
intangible asset
無形資産、無体資産
(特許権、商標権など)
intangible reward
無形報酬
intangible value
無形価額
integrated circuit
集積回路、ＩＣ
integration, backward
後方統合、後向きの統合
integration, forward
順方向統合
integration, horizontal
水平統合
integration, vertical
縦の統合
integrity
完全性、インテグリティー

interactive
対話形の、会話形の、
インターアクティブの
interactive system
対話形システム
interest
利害関係、利権、利子
interest group
利益集団、利益者集団、
インタレストグループ
interest-only loan
当座の支払債務が利子のみで元金の支払は据置かれる方式の貸付金（融資）
interest rate
利子率、利率
interest sensitive policies
金利連動型保険証券
interface
インターフェイス、接続器、相異なる装置を接続するための仲介装置、
interim audit
中間監査、期中監査
interim financing
中間資金調達
interim statement
中間計算書
interindustry competition
産業間競争
interlocking directorate
兼任重役会
interlocutory decree
中間判決、暫定的判決
intermediary
中間の、媒介の、仲介者
intermediate goods
中間財
intermediate term
中期
intermediation
仲介、中継売買
intermittent production
断続生産
internal audit
内部監査
internal check
内部牽制
internal control
内部統制
internal expansion
内部膨張、内部拡大
internal financing
内部金融
internal memory
内部記憶装置、
内部メモリー
internal modem
内臓モデム
internal rate of return (IRR)
内部収益率
Internal Revenue Service (IRS)
米国内国歳入庁
International Bank for Reconstruction and Development
国際復興開発銀行

international cartel
国際カルテル
international law
国際法
International Monetary Fund
国際通貨基金
International Monetary Market
国際通貨市場
international union
国際的連盟、国際的組合
internet
インターネット
internet protocol (IP) address
インターネット
プロトコルアドレス、
ＩＰ住所
internet service provider
インターネット
サービス提供者
interperiod income tax allocation
所得課税の期間を跨っての
配分
interpleader
競合権利者確定手続
interpolation
加筆、改竄、挿入
interpreter
解釈者、通訳、
通訳官
interrogatories
質問、質問書
interval scale
間隔尺度、単位尺度
interview
会見、面談、面接
interview, structured
定形会見（面談、面接）
interview, unstructured
非定形会見（面談、面接）
interview basis
会見の基本
interstate
州間
in the money
金持ちで、インザマネーで
in the tank
インザタンク、
市価の急落
intraperiod tax allocation
所得課税の期間内配分
intrinsic value
本源的価値、真性価値、
本質価値
insure
保証する、に保険をつける、
を保険に入れる
inventory
棚卸資産、在庫品、
在庫調べ
inventory certificate
棚卸証明書
inventory control
在庫管理、在庫品管理、
棚卸管理
inventory financing
在庫品金融

inventory planning
在庫計画
inventory shortage (shrinkage)
在庫不足
inventory turnover
棚卸資産回転率
inverted yield curve
逆利回り曲線
invest
投資する、運用する、授ける
investment
投資
investment advisory service
投資顧問サービス
investment banker
投資金融業者
investment club
投資クラブ
investment company
投資会社、投資信託会社
investment counsel
投資相談
investment grade
投資等級
investment interest expense
投資利息費用
investment life cycle
投資寿命
investment strategy
投資戦略
investment trust
投資信託
investor relations department
投資家関係担当部課
invoice
仕入状、請求書
involuntary conversion
強制交換
involuntary lien
強制留置権、強制先取特権
involuntary trust
強制信託
involuntary unemployment
非自発的失業
Inwood annuity factor
インウッド年金要素、インウッド年金要因
iota
少量、微量
irregulars
傷物、規則外の品
irreparable harm, irreparable damage
回復不能の損害
irretrievable
検索不能な
irrevocable
取消不能な、撤回不能の
irrevocable trust
取消不能信託
issue
出す、振り出し、問題
issued and outstanding
振出済みで未払いの
issuer
発行者、振出人

itemized deductions
項目別控除額、
明細控除額

iteration
反復

itinerant worker
渡り労働者、移動労働者

J

jawboning
ジョーボーニング、
強制的説得工作

J-curve
Ｊカーブ

job
仕事、職務

job bank
人材銀行、
ジョブバンク

jobber
仲買人、手間賃人夫

job classification
職階制、職務分類

job cost sheet
個別原価計算書、
作業指図書別原価計算表

job depth
作業深度

job description
職務(職種)記載書、
職務説明書

job evaluation
職務評価

job jumper
職場を転々と変える人

job lot
取引口、
込み売りの廉価品、規格はずれ品

job order
(作業員に対する)作業指令票、作業票

job placement
職業紹介、就業斡旋、
作業の配置、

job rotation
職場の配置転換

job satisfaction
仕事の満足度

job security
雇用保証

job sharing
仕事分配

job shop
ジョブショップ
(短期雇用契約で働く人を斡旋する職業紹介機関)

job specification
職場(職務)の明細書または説明書

job ticket
作業票(労働者に対して配布される)

joint account
共同勘定、共同口座、

joint and several liability
連帯的債務

joint and survivor annuity
共同生存者年金

joint fare, joint rate
結合運賃、結合料率
joint liability
共同責任
jointly and severally
連帯的に
joint product cost
共同製品原価
joint return
共同申告
joint stock company
法人格のない株式会社[株式社団]、(英)株式会社
joint tendency
合有不動産権
joint venture
合弁事業、
ジョイントベンチャー
journal
仕訳帳
journal entry
仕訳記入
journalize
(勘定を)仕訳する、
を仕訳帳に記入する
journal voucher
仕訳伝票
journeymen
職人、(平凡な仕事分野の)熟練者、下働きをする人
judgment
判決、判断
judgment creditor
判決債権者
judgment debtor
判決債務者
judgment lien
判決先取特権
judgment proof
紙切れ判決、
判決執行不能の
judgment sample
有意見本
judicial bond
裁判保障
judicial foreclosure or judicial sale
司法上の譲渡抵当実行手続き、
または司法上の売却
jumbo certificate of deposit
ジャンボ預金証書
junior issue
下位証券
junior lien
下位先取権、下位留置権
junior mortgage
後順位抵当
junior partner
下級社員
junior security
下位証券、下位担保
junk bond
ジャンクボンド、
ジャンク債
jurisdiction
裁判権、管轄権、管轄区域
jurisprudence
法律学、法理学
jury
陪審
just compensation
当然の（正当な）補償

justifiable
正当と認められる、もっともな

justified price
正当だと認められた価格

K

Keogh plan
キオプラン、米国の自営業者退職年金制度
key
キー
key-area evaluation
重要地域評価
keyboard
キーボード
key person life and health insurance
経営者保険、企業幹部保険
kickback
不当手数料、(賃金などの)ピンはね、返答
kicker
追加的コスト、インセンティブ(証券などに付随する追加的特権)、以外な結末
kiddie tax
14歳未満の未成年者の投資収入に対する税金（親が申告する）
killing
殺すこと、（株などでの）ぼろもうけ、大もうけ
kiting
（小切手の）過振り、融通手形（空手形）を振り出すこと
know-how
ノウハウ、実際的な知識、技術
knowledge intensive
知識集中的な、知識集約的な
know-your-customer rule
顧客を良く知るという原則
kudos
栄光、名声、賞賛

L

labeling laws
法律のラベルを付けること
labor
労働、労力
labor agreement
労働協約
labor dispute
労働争議
labor force
労働人口、労働力
labor intensive
労働集約的
labor mobility
労働の移動性、
労働移動性
labor piracy
労働争奪
labor pool
労働プール
labor union
労働組合
laches
権利行使の懈怠
lading
荷を積むこと、船積み
lagging indicator
遅行指標
LAN (local area network)
ラン、構内ネットワーク、
LAN
land
陸、陸地、土地
land banking
土地抵当貸銀行業、
土地担保貸銀行業、
land contract
土地延べ払い契約
land development
土地開発
landlocked
陸地に囲まれた、
内陸の
landlord
地主、家主、
アパート経営者
landmark
陸標、陸上の目印、
歴史的建造物
landscape (format)
横向き（形式）
land trust
土地信託
land-use intensity
土地利用集約度
land-use planning
土地利用計画
land-use
regulation
土地利用規制

land-use succession
土地利用相続（権）
lapping
たらい回し（売掛金の）
lapse
保険契約の失効、
権利特権の消滅、失効
lapsing schedule
固定資産増減明細表
last in, first out (LIFO)
後入先出法
last sale
最終売上げ
latent defect
潜在欠陥
latitude
緯度、自由の範囲、許容度
law
法、法律、法令
law of diminishing returns
収穫逓減の法則
law of increasing costs
生産費漸増の法則
law of large numbers
（統計）大数の法則
law of supply and demand
供給と需要の法則
lay off
レイオフ、一時解雇、
一時的強制休業
leader
指揮者、指導者
leader pricing
花形銘柄価格決定
leading indicators
先駆指標、先行指標
lead time
リードタイム、準備期間
lease
借受証、借用契約、
貸借契約期間
leasehold
賃借権、定期賃借権
leasehold improvement
借地借家加工改良費
leasehold insurance
賃貸保険
leasehold mortgage
賃貸抵当、賃貸抵当権
leasehold value
賃貸価値
lease with option to purchase
購買選択権付き賃貸
least-effort principle
最小努力の原理
leave of absence
休職（休暇、休学）許可
ledger
元帳、台帳
legal entity
法的実体、法的組織体
legal investment
法的投資
legal list
法定銘柄
legal monopoly
合法的独占、法定独占
legal name
（正式）氏名
legal notice
適法な通知

legal opinion
裁判官（裁判所）の意見（評価，判定）
legal right
法的権利
legal tender
法定通貨、本位貨幣
legal wrong
法的な誤り、法的不正
legatee
遺産受取人、被遺贈者
lender
(コール資金の）出し手、貸方
lessee
賃借人
lessor
賃貸人、貸主
less than carload (L/C)
一両分の貨車より少ない
letter of intent
契約意図表明書
letter stock
投資目的確認書付株式、売却制限株式
level debt service
負債均等化サービス
level out
均等にする、均一化する
level-payment income stream
定額年金の定期的支払い
level-payment mortgage
定額支払抵当
level premium
平準保険料
leverage
レバリッジ、影響力
leveraged buyout (LBO)
レバリッジ・バイアウト，LBO 式企業買収
leveraged company
レバレッジド会社　（利益を見越して資金を借り入れた）
leveraged lease
レバレッジド・リース
levy
課税、徴税
liability
責任、負担義務、負担額
liability, business exposures
事業の経済的リスクの責任（負債）
liability, civil
民事責任
liability, criminal
刑事責任
liability dividend
責任配当
liability insurance
（賠償）責任保険、損害賠償保険、
liability, legal
法定責任
liability, professional
専門職業責任
liable
(法律上の、または負債・損害などに対し）責任がある、(…する)義務がある、(返済に)当てられる

libel
文書誹毀、文書誹毀罪
license
許可（書）、認可（書）、免許（状）、使用許諾（書）
license bond
免許(認可)債券、認可証債務証書
licensee
許可(認可、許諾、免許)を受けた者、被許可者
license law
免許法
licensing examination
免許(認可、許諾)審査
lien
先取特権、留置権
life cycle
ライフサイクル、生活循環
life estate
生涯不動産権
life expectancy
平均余命、平均余命数
life tenant
終身借地人、終身財産使用権者
lighterage
はしけ運搬、はしけ(使用)料
like-kind property
同種類の財産（所有物、不動産）、特性（属性、固有性）
limited audit
限定監査
limited company
有限責任会社
limited distribution
限定分配（配給、配当、分布）
limited liability
有限責任
limited occupancy agreement
限定占有居住の合意、限定居住の合意
limited or special partner
有限責任社員、有限責任組合員
limited partnership
有限責任会社、有限責任組合、合資会社、
limited payment life insurance
有限払込み生命保険
limit order
指値付き注文
limit up, limit down
ストップ高、ストップ安
line
列、在庫品、保険（ある種の）
line and staff organization
ラインスタッフ組織、参謀部制直系組織
line authority
ラインの権威（権限，当局）

line control
ライン管理、ライン制御
line extension
ライン拡張
line function
ライン機能
line management
ライン経営、ライン管理

line of credit
信用限度
line organization
直系組織、ライン組織
line pitch
行ピッチ
line printer
ラインプリンター
link
相互連絡、リンクする、連結する
linked object
リンク（相互連結）したオブジェクト
liquid asset
流動資産
liquidate
清算する、支払う、弁済する
liquidated damages
確定賠償額
liquidated debt
確定額債務
liquidated value
清算価額
liquidation
清算、換金、解散
liquidation dividend
清算配当
liquid crystal display (LCD)
液晶ディスプレイ、LCD
liquidity
流動性、換金性
liquidity preference
流動性選好
liquidity ratio
流動性比率
list
目録、表
listed options
上場オプション
listed security
上場株式（証券）
listing
不動産業者の土地家屋仲介権（契約）、
(証券の）上場、表・
名簿などの作成、表・
名簿などに記載されること
listing agent, listing broker
（不動産取扱物件の）リスト掲載仲介業者、
上場代理人、上場ブローカー
listing requirements
上場審査基準
list price
表示価格
litigant
訴訟当事者
litigation
訴訟
living trust
生前信託

load
付加料、保険料に付加する
load fund
ロードファンド、
手数料負荷投資信託（ミューチュアルファンドなど）
loan
貸付、借入、融資、ローン
loan application
貸付申込み、融資申込み、
ローン申込み
loan committee
貸付委員会、融資委員会
loan-to-value ratio (LTV)
評価価格融資率
loan value
貸付価値
lobbyist
ロビイスト、
院外活動家
lock box
ロックボックス、鍵付の箱
locked in
固定した、確定した
lockout
労働者締め出し、工場閉鎖、事業所閉鎖、ロックアウト
lock-up option
固定オプション、ロックアップ・オプション
logic diagram
論理図
log in (log on)
ログイン（ログオン）、
接続開始、ネットワークシステムにアクセスする
login identification (login ID)
IDをログインする
logo
ロゴ、社名・商品名などを図案化した文字、
ロゴマーク
log off
ログオフする、コンピューターの使用を終了する
long bond
長期債券
long coupon
長期クーポン
longevity pay
年功加給、年功加俸
long position
買い超、買持ちポジション、
ロングポジション
long-range planning
長期計画
long-term debt or long-term liability
長期借入金または長期債務
long-term gain (loss)
長期収益（損失）
long-term trend
長期的趨勢
long-wave cycle
長期波動循環
loop
輪、輪形のもの、環
loophole
空気抜き、抜け穴
loosen rein
統制を緩める

loss
欠損、損失、穴
（欠損）
loss adjustment expense
損失修正（調整、補正）
費用
loss carryback
繰戻欠損金
loss carryforward
繰越欠損金
loss contingency
損失偶発事件
loss leader
目玉商品、おとり商品
loss of income insurance
所得損失保険
loss ratio
損害率
lot and block
ロット・アンド・ブロック、
一口と大口（の株）
lot line
用地境界線

lottery
抽選、富くじ
low
低い、安い
lower case character/letter
下段文字、小文字
lower-involvement model
係わり合いの少ないモデル
lower of cost or market
原価又は市価の低いほう
low-grade
低等級、低品位、低格付け
low resolution
低解像度
low-tech
ローテク
（低レベルの工業技術）
lump sum
一括、一括払い、総金額
lump sum distribution
一括配賦、一括分配
lump-sum purchase
一括購入
luxury tax
ぜいたく品税，奢侈税

M

macro
マクロ
macroeconomics
巨視的経済学、
マクロ経済学
macroenvironment
巨視的環境
magnetic card
磁気カード
magnetic strip
磁気ストリップ
mailbox
（電子メールの）
メールボックス、
ポスト
mail fraud
郵便物詐欺
mailing list
郵送リスト、
郵送一覧表
mainframe
メーンフレーム、
大型汎用コンピューター
main menu
メインメニュー
maintenance
維持、扶養、生計
maintenance bond
扶養保証
maintenance fee
維持費、管理費
maintenance method
維持法、管理法
majority
過半数、大多数
majority shareholder
株主の過半数
maker
製作者、メーカー、
製造業者
make-work
人を雇う為に作る仕事、
労働者をあそばせないため
に作る仕事
malicious mischief
故意の器物損壊
malingerer
（任務回避のために）
仮病を使う者
malingering
仮病を使うこと
mall
モール、
プロムナード風商店街、
ショッピングセンター
malpractice
医療過誤、弁護過誤、
（専門家の）業務過誤

manage
管理する、運営（経営）する、監督する
managed account
管理会計
managed currency
管理通貨、統制貨幣
managed economy
管理経済
management
経営、管理、
経営者側
management agreement
経営委託契約
management audit
経営監査
management by crisis
危機による管理
management by exception
例外による管理
management by objective (MBO)
目的による管理
management by walking around (MBWA)
歩き回り管理、
視察案内型経営
management consultant
経営コンサルタント、
マネジメントコンサルタント
management cycle
管理サイクル
management fee
幹事手数料
management game
経営管理ゲーム
management guide
経営管理ガイド
management information system (MIS)
経営情報システム、
経営情報管理制度
management prerogative
経営特権
management ratio
経営比率
management science
経営科学
management style
経営スタイル、経営様式
management system
経営システム、
管理システム
manager
支配人、経営者、部長
managerial accounting
管理会計
managerial grid
経営グリッド、
経営管理の配列網
mandate
指令、職務執行令状、依託（代理）
mandatory copy
強制的コピー
man-hour
（延べ）労働時間、工数
manifest
宣言、声明書、積荷目録

manipulation
巧妙な取扱い、市場操作、あやつり相場

manual
手の、提要、手引き

manual skill
器用さ（技能、技術、わざ）

manufacture
製造（する）、生産（する）

manufacturing cost
製造原価、製造費

manufacturing inventory
製造棚卸資産（在庫、在庫品）

manufacturing order
製造指図書

map
地図、図

margin
限界、最低収益点、差額、（株式の）証拠金

margin account
証拠金勘定

marginal cost
限界原価、限界費用

marginal cost curve
限界費用曲線

marginal efficiency of capital
資本の限界効率

marginal producer
限界生産者

marginal propensity to consume (MPC)
限界消費性向

marginal propensity to invest
限界投資性向

marginal propensity to save (MPS)
限界貯蓄性向

marginal property
限界財産、限界所有物、限界不動産

marginal revenue
限界収入

marginal tax rate
限界税率

marginal utility
限界効用

margin call
追加証拠金

margin of profit
利ざや、採算

margin of safety
安全余裕率

margins
利ざや、証拠金、限界収益点

marital deduction
婚姻控除

markdown
マークダウン、価格引下げ、値段引き下げ

market
市場、売買、市価

marketability
市場性
marketable securities
有価証券、
市場性のある証券
marketable title
売買に適する権利
market aggregation
市場合算
market analysis
市場分析
market area
市場地域
market basket
マーケットバスケット（方式）
market comparison approach
市場比較手法
market demand
市場需要
market development index
市場開発指数
market economy
市場経済
market equilibrium
市場均衡
market index
市場指数
marketing
マーケティング、市場取引
marketing concept
マーケティングコンセプト、
マーケティング志向
market director
市場担当取締役、
市場担当理事
marketing information system
マーケティング戦略情報システム、市場情報システム
marketing mix
マーケティングミックス
marketing plan
マーケティング計画
marketing research
マーケティング調査、
市場調査
market letter
市場案内、市況レポート
market order
成行き注文、市価取引注文
market penetration
市場浸透
market price
市場価格、相場、時価
market rent
市場超過利潤
market research
市場調査
market segmentation
市場細分化
market share
マーケットシェア、
市場占拠率、
市場占有率
market system
市場組織
market test
市場試験

market timing
市場タイミング
market value
市場価格
market value clause
市場価格条項
mark to the market
値洗い
markup
値上げ
marriage penalty
婚姻罰金
Marxism
マルクス主義
mask
マスク
mass appeal
大衆の心を捉える
（魅了する）
mass communication
大衆伝達、マスコミ
mass media
マスメディア、大衆媒体
mass production
大量生産、マスプロ、量産
master boot record
マスタ起動記録
master lease
マスターリース、
基本賃借権
master limited partnership
基本有限会社
master plan
マスタープラン、
基本計画
master policy
一括保険証券
master-servant rule
雇用規則、雇用関係規則
masthead
発行人欄、マストの先端
matching principle
対応の原則
material
材料、資料、
原料
material fact
重要な事実
materiality
重要性
materialman
資材供給業者
materials handling
資材取扱い
materials management
原材料の管理
matrix
マトリックス、母体、原版
matrix organization
マトリックス編成（組織、
体制、機構）
matured endowment
満期になった基金
（養老資金、養老保険）
mature economy
成熟経済
maturity
成熟、満期、
成熟期
maturity date
満期日、支払期日、返済日

maximize
最大限にする、最大化する、極大化する
maximum capacity
最大能力、最大容量、最大収容能力
m-cats
医学大学入学テスト
mean, arithmetic
算術平均
mean, geometric
幾何平均
mean return
平均利益
mechanic's lien
建築工事に関するリーエン（先取権）
mechanization
機械化
media
媒体、手段、情報伝達媒体、
media buy
メディア買い、メディア購買、媒体購入
media buyer
メディアバイヤー、媒体セールス担当
media option
メディアオプション
media plan
媒体計画
media planner
メディアプランナー、メディア計画者
media player
ミディアプレイヤー
mediation
仲介、調停、仲裁
media weight
メディアウェイト
medical examination
身体検査、健康診断
medium
中間の、中間物、媒体、手段
medium of exchange
交換手段
medium-term bond
中期債券
meeting of minds
意見の一致、見解の完全な一致
megabucks
100万ドル、大金、何百万ドルもの金
megatype
メガタイプ、巨大タイプ
member bank
会員銀行、加盟銀行、組合銀行
member firm or corporation
会員業者または会社
memorandum
メモ、覚書き、売買覚書き
memory
記憶（力）、記憶の範囲、記憶装置

memory (computer)
記憶装置、メモリー
menial
卑しい、下賤な、
みすぼらしい
menu bar
メニューバー
mercantile
商人の、商業の、商売の
mercantile agency
商事代理
mercantile law
商事法、商業法、商法
mercantilism
マーカンティリズム、
重商主義、商業本位
merchandise
商品、物品、製品
merchandise allowance
商品準備金、商品引当金、
商品控除
merchandise broker
商品ブローカー、
商品仲介業者
merchandise control
商品管理、商品統制
merchandising
取引、商品化計画、
流通業
merchandising director
マーチャンダイジング担当取締役、商品化計画担当取締役
merchandising service
マーチャンダイジング
サービス
merchantable
市場性のある、市場向きの
merchant bank
マーチャントバンク、
証券引受銀行
merge
合併（併合）する、結合する、吸収される
merger
合同、吸収合併、
合併する人（もの）
merit increase
価値（業績，長所）の増大
merit rating
人事考査、勤務評定、
能力考査
meter rate
メーター料金（代金）、
計測料金
metes and bounds
境界、境界線、境界石
methods, time measurement (MTM)
時間測定方法
metrication
メートル法化、
メートル法移行
metric system
メートル法
metropolitan
area
大都市圏、
首都圏
microeconomics
微視的経済学、
ミクロ経済学

micromotion study
微少時間の微細動作研究、
微細動作分析
midcareer plateau
履歴半ばの安定状態、
経歴半ばの停滞期（状態）
middle management
中間管理者、中間管理層、
ミドルマネージメント
midnight deadline
真夜中締切り、
午前0時締切り
migrate
（ファイルなどを）
移動させる
migratory worker
季節労働者
military-industrial complex
軍産複合体制
milking
搾乳、搾り出すこと、
搾取すること、
（情報などを）
milking strategy
搾乳戦略
mileage rate
1ドル当たり1000分の1
の課税率
millionaire
百万長者、大金持ち、
大富豪
millionaire on paper
紙の上だけの百万長者、名
目だけの百万長者
mineral rights
鉱業（採掘）権
minimax principle
ミニマックスの原理、
最少最大原理
minimize
アイコン化する、
ミニマイズ
minimum lease payments
最低額リース支払
minimum lot area
最小区画地域
minimum pension liability
最低年金債務
minimum premium deposit plan
最低保険料供託金方式
minimum wage
最低賃金
minor
未成年者、少数の、
重要でない
minority interest or minority investment
少数株主持分、少数株主権、
またはマイノリティー投資
mintage
貨幣鋳造、造幣
minutes
議事録
misdemeanor
軽罪
mismanagement
管理（経営）を誤ること、
管理失敗
misrepresentation
不実表示、
虚偽の表示

misstatement of age
年齢の誤った陳述、
年齢の偽りの申立て
mistake
誤り、間違い、誤解
mistake of law
法律の錯誤
mitigation of damages
損害賠償額の軽減
mix
混ぜる、混合、混乱
mixed economy
混合経済
mixed perils
混合危険（保険）
mixed signals
混合信号、混沌とした合図、
まちまちの市況
mode
方法、様式、モード
modeling
モデリング、モデル化、
模型製作
modeling language
モデル化言語
model unit
モデル単位、モデル装置
modern portfolio theory (MPT)
現代ポートフォリオ理論
modified accrual
修正未収支勘定
modified life insurance
修正生命保険
modified union shop
修正ユニオンショップ
module
モジュール、
交換可能な構成部分
mom and pop store
夫婦経営商店、
小規模小売店
momentum
はずみ、勢い、運動量
monetarist
マネタリスト、通貨主義者
monetary
貨幣の、通貨の、金融上の
monetary item
金銭項目
monetary reserve
通貨準備金
monetary standard
貨幣標準
money
金、通貨
money illusion
貨幣錯覚、
マネーイリュージョン
money income
貨幣所得
money market
マネーマーケット、
（短期）金融市場
money market fund
短期金融資産ファンド、
短期金融資産投資信託
money supply
マネーサプライ、
通貨供給量、
貨幣供給量

monopolist
独占者、独占論者、
独占企業
monopoly
独占、独占権、
独占企業
monopoly price
独占価格
monopsony
需要独占、購買者独占、
買手独占
monthly compounding of interest
毎月利子を福利計算すること
monthly investment plan
月次利子計画
month-to-month tenancy
月決め借用（借家人、
居住人）
monument
記念建造物、モニュメント、
重要遺物
moonlighting
夜間副業をすること
morale
士気、風紀
moral hazard
道徳的危険、
モラル・
ハザード
moral law
道徳律
moral obligation bond
道義的支払保証債券
moral suasion
道徳に訴える勧告、
道徳的勧告
moratorium
支払停止、支払猶予、
支払猶予期間
mortality table
死亡表、死亡率統計表
mortgage
譲渡抵当権、抵当権、
抵当に入れる
mortgage assumption
抵当権引受け
mortgage-backed certificate
モーゲージ担保証書
mortgage-backed security
モーゲージ担保証券
mortgage banker
譲渡抵当権金融会社、
抵当銀行
mortgage bond
モーゲージ付債券、
担保付き債券
mortgage broker
モーゲージブローカー、譲
渡抵当権仲買人
mortgage commitment
譲渡抵当権売買約定(約束)
mortgage constant
モーゲージ定数（常数）
mortgage correspondent
モーゲージ通信者（取引
先）、抵当権取引店
mortgage debt
不動産抵当負債、抵当借

mortgage discount
抵当割引
mortgagee
譲渡抵当権者、抵当債券者
mortgage insurance
抵当保険
mortgage insurance policy
抵当保険証券、
抵当保険証書、
抵当保険契約
mortgage lien
抵当リーエン、
抵当先取権、抵当留置権
mortgage out
譲渡抵当権アウト、
モーゲージアウト
mortgage relief
抵当救済、
抵当除去
mortgage servicing
抵当ローンの提供
mortgagor
抵当権設定者
motion study
動作研究
motivation
動機、動機づけ
motor freight
自動車貨物、
自動車運送賃
mouse
マウス
mouse pad
マウスパッド
movement
動き、変動、動向
mover and shaker
実力者、有力者、大者
moving average
移動平均
muckraker
醜聞あさり、醜聞を暴く人、
醜聞記事を記載する新聞雑誌
multibuyer
複数バイヤー、多数購入者
multicasting
マルチキャスティング
multicollinearity
多数共直線性
multiemployer bargaining
統一団体交渉
multifunction
多重機能
multimedia
（多様な伝達手段・宣伝媒体を持つ）マルチメディア、
多元媒体
multinational corporation (MNC)
多国籍企業
multiple
多数の、多量の、
複合の
multiple listing
複数リスト
multiple locations forms
複数所在地書式

multiple-management plan
複合経営計画、
複層管理計画、
多角経営計画
multiple-peril insurance
複合危機保険
multiple regression
多重回帰
multiple retirement ages
複合退職年齢
multiple shop
連鎖店、チェーンストア
multiplier
乗数
multiuser
マルチユーザー、
多数利用者
municipal bond
地方債
municipal revenue bond
市特定財源債、
地方特定財源債券
muniments of title
不動産権利証書
mutual association
相互組合、相互協会
mutual company
相互会社
mutual fund
ミューチュアルファンド、
オープンエンド型投資資金、
投資信託
mutual insurance company
相互保険会社
mutuality of contract
契約の相互性

N

naked option
ネーキッドオプション、無権利オプションファンド
naked position
ネーキッドポジション、無権利所有
named peril policy
特定危険保険
name position bond
記名式地位身元信用債権
name schedule bond
記名式明細書付信用債権
nationalization
国有化、国民化、国営
national wealth
国富
natural business year
自然営業年度、自然年度
natural monopoly
自然独占
natural resources
天然資源、自然資源
（土地、鉱物、水）
navigation
ナビゲーション、移動
near money
ニヤーマネー、近似通貨、準貨幣
need satisfaction
ニーズ充足、必要充足
negative amortization
(借入元本の）負の償却、逆償還
negative carry
ネガティブキャリー
negative cash flow
マイナスキャッシュフロー、現金流出
negative correlation
逆相関、負の相関
negative income tax
負の所得税、逆所得税
negative working capital
負の営業資本、負の運転資本
negligence
怠慢、不注意な行為、過失
negotiable
交渉の余地のある、交渉できる、譲渡可能の

negotiable certificate of deposit
譲渡可能定期預金証書
negotiable instrument
流通証券
negotiable order of withdrawal (NOW)
譲渡可能払戻し指図
negotiated market price
相対市場価格、顧客市場価格
negotiated price
相対価格、交渉価格
negotiation
交渉、商議、取引
neighborhood store
近所の店、近隣の店舗
neoclassical economics
新古典派経済学
nepotism
縁者びいき、親族登用、縁故者のコネ
nest egg
種銭、予備金、蓄え
net
正味の、正価の、最終的な
net assets
純財産、純資産
net asset value (NAV)
純資産価値
net book value
正味帳簿価額
net contribution
正味掛金、正味拠出金、正味分担金
net cost
純原価
net current assets
正味流動資産
net income
純所得、純利益、純益
net income per share of common stock
普通株の一株（一口）当たりの純益
net leasable area
純賃借可能地域
net lease
ネットリース（賃借人が諸経費を負担する賃貸借契約）
net listing
手取額指定仲介
net loss
純損失、正味支払保険金
net national product
国民純生産、純国民生産物
net operation income (NOI)
純営業収益
net operating loss (NOL)
純営業損失
net present value (NPV)
純現在価値
net proceeds
正味売上高、純売上高、純手取金
net profit
純益
net profit margin
売上純利益限界

net purchases
純仕入高、純購入高、
正味仕入高
net quick assets
正味当座資産
net rate
正味料率
net realizable value
(資産評価の)
正味実現可能価額
net sales
正味売上高、純売上高
net surfing
ネットサーフィン
net transaction
正味取引
network
ネットワーク
network administrator
ネットワーク管理者、
ネットワークアドミニスト
レーター
networking
ネットワーキング、ネット
ワーク作り
net yield
純利回り、税引利回り
new issue
新規発売
new money
ニューマネー、新規貨幣、
新規資金
newspaper syndicate
ニュースペーパーシンジケ
ート、新聞企業連合、
新聞記事配給業者
new town
ニュータウン、新都市、
大住宅団地
niche
ニッチ、特定市場分野、市
場のすき間
night letter
夜間（発送）電報、
overnight telegram の旧称
node
ノード、節点、結節点

no-growth
ゼロ成長
no-load fund
ノーロードファンド、（手
数料無料の）ミューチュア
ルファンド、直売ミューチ
ュアルファンド
nominal account
名目勘定、仮勘定
nominal damages
名目的損害賠償金
nominal interest rate
表面金利、名目金利,
表面利子率
nominal scale
名義尺度
nominal wage
名目賃金
nominal yield
名目利回り
nominee
推薦された人、
候補に指名された人、
受取人、名義人

noncallable
（債券が）
繰上げ償還のできない、
満期償還の
noncompetitive bid
非競争入札
nonconforming use
不適合利用
noncontestability clause
不可争条項
noncumulative preferred stock
非累積型優先株式
noncurrent asset
非流動資産、
固定資産
nondeductibility of employer contributions
控除不可能雇用者分担金
（企業拠出金）、
非控除雇用者分担金
nondiscretionary trust
限定信託
nondisturbance clause
権利不侵害条項
nondurable goods
非耐久財、非耐久消費財
nonformatted
書式化されていない
nonglare
ノングレア、反射防止
nonmember bank
非加盟銀行、組合外銀行、
ノンメンバーバンク
nonmember firm
非会員会社、組合外商会
nonmonetary item
非貨幣項目
nonnegotiable instrument
譲渡不能証券
nonoperating expense (revenue)
営業外費用（収益）
nonparametric statistics
ノンパラメトリック統計
nonperformance
不履行
nonproductive
非生産的
nonproductive loan
非生産的融資
nonprofit accounting
非営利会計
nonprofit corporation
非営利会社、非営利企業
nonpublic information
非公開情報
nonrecourse
ノンリコース、第二次的請
求権放棄の
nonrecurring charge
臨時経費
nonrefundable
返金不可の、払戻し不能の
nonrefundable fee or nonrefundable deposit
払戻し不能手数料、
払戻し不能予約金

nonrenewable natural resources
再生不能の天然資源
nonstock corporation
非株式法人
nonstore retailing
無店舗販売
nonvoting stock
無議決権株
non-par stock
無額面株、額面未詳株
norm
標準、ノルマ、
責任生産量
normal price
正常価格、平準価格
normal profit
正常利潤、正常利益
normal retirement age
通常退職年齢
normal wear and tear
正常損耗、通常の摩滅
normative economics
規範的経済学
no-strike clause
非ストライキ条項、
非同盟罷業条項
notarize
<証書・契約などを>
(公証人を通して)公証する、
証明させる
note
覚書、ノート、手形
notebook computer
ノート（型）パソコン、
ノートブックサイズの携帯
コンピューター
note payable
支払手形
note receivable
受取手形
not for profit
非営利、非営利の
notice
通知、通告、通知書
notice of cancellation clause
解約予告条項、
解約通知条項
notice of default
債務不履行通知
notice of quit
解約予告、辞職勧告
not rated (nr)
見積もられなかった、
評価されなかった、
課税評価されていない
novation
(債務・契約などの)更改、
更新、刷新、革新
NSF （NOT SUFFICIENT
FUND の略）：資金不足、
残高不足
nuisance
迷惑な人・物・こと・
行為など、生活妨害
null and void
(法律上)無効の
num lock key
数値ロックキー

O

objective
目的、客観的な、目的の
objective value
客観的価値、
客観価値説
obligation bond
公債、社債
obligee
債権者
obligor
債務者
observation test
立会検査
obsolescence
老朽、衰微、旧式化
occupancy level
居住・財産占有・
（所有物の）利用の程度・
度合
occupancy, occupant
財産占有、使用；占有者、
現住者
occupation
業務、仕事、職業
occupational analysis
職業分析
occupational disease
職業的疾病、職業病,
業務上の疾病
occupational group
職業集団
occupational hazard
職業上の危険
odd lot
半端もの、端数、端株
odd page
奇数ページ
odd-value pricing
端数価格設定
offer
申し出る、売りに出す、
売買の申込み
offer and acceptance
申し込みと引受け
offeree
申込みの相手方、
被申込人
offerer
申込者
offering date
申込期日
offering price
申込価格
office management
事務管理
official exchange rate
公定為替相場、
公定交換比率

off-line
オフライン、非直結
off peak
オフピーク、
混雑していない時間帯
off-price
割引販売の、安売りの
off-sale date
売残品引き取り日
offset
差引勘定の等しいもの、
埋め合わせ、釣り合う
offshore
海外の、沖合で、国外での
off-site cost
オフサイトコスト、
敷地外での価格
off the balance sheet
貸借対照表外の
off the books
記録から消されて、（法律などが）廃止されて、
除名されて
off time
暇な時間、閑散時、
不景気な時
oil and gas lease
オイルガスリース、石油・ガスを採掘する権利を与える借地契約
oligopoly
少数独占、寡占
ombudsman
オンブズマン
omitted dividend
無配
on account
掛売り、内払い、信用で
onboard computer
搭載コンピューター
on demand
要求払いで、一覧払いで、
参着払いで、
one-cent sale
１銭セール
one-hundred-percent location
百分率所在地
one-minute manager
「ワン・ミニット・マネージャー」
（本のタイトル）
one-time buyer
単発購入者
one-time rate
単発料金
on-line
オンライン、直結
on-line data base
オンラインデータベース
on order
(品物が)発注済みの、
注文中の
on-sale date
販売日
on speculation (on spec)
投機で
on-the-job training (OJT)
職場内教育、職場内訓練、
職場訓練

open
開いた、開放した、公開の、未定の

open account
オープン勘定、掛売買勘定、掛売買取引、未決算勘定

open bit
公開入札

open dating
日付表示制度、（食品の）鮮度保証期限の表示

open distribution
オープンディストリビューション

open-door policy
門戸開放政策、自由貿易政策、オープンドア方式

open economy
開放経済

open-end
(担保、契約などが)開放式の、資本額の可変的な、無期限の

open-end lease
リース物件の交換自由なリース

open-end management company
開放型経営会社

open-end mortgage
開放型担保付き社債

open house
一般公開、工場公開、自宅開放、

open housing
公正住宅販売政策

opening
開く（あける）こと、始まり、［証券］寄り付き

open interest
オープンインタレスト、（売り手側の／買手側の）建玉

open listing
開放式委任契約

open-market rates
市中金利

open mortgage
総括抵当権

open order
見計らい注文、市価注文、無条件注文、保留注文

open outcry
オープンアウトクライ方式、公開セリ売買方式

open shop
オープンショップ、労働組合への加入が任意で、それが雇用の条件にはならない事業所・企業またはその労使間協定

open space
オープンスペース、空地、広場

open stock
バラ買いできる補充商品、セット商品

open-to-buy
購買余力、発注残高

open union
公開組合

operand
演算数
operating cycle
営業周期
operating expense
営業費用、作業費用、運転費用
operating lease
営業リース
operating loss
営業損失、操業損失、業務損失
operating profit (loss)
営業利潤（損失）、操業利潤（損失）、業務利益（損失）
operating ratio
営業比率、操業度、操業率
operating system
オペレーティングシステム、基本ソフトウエア
operational audit
業務監査
operational control
運転統制、作業統制、業務管理
operation mode
操作モード
operations research (OR)
作戦研究、経営研究
operator
操作員、演算子、オペレーター
opinion
意見、見解、世論
opinion leader
世論指導者、世論の担い手、世論形成者
opinion of title
不動産権原の弁護士意見書
opportunity cost
機会費用、機会原価
optical character recognition (OCR)
光学式文字認識
optical fiber
光ファイバー、光学繊維、オプティカルファイバー
optimum capacity
最適能力
option
選択権、（売付買付）選択権、選択
optional modes of settlement
（保険金などの）支払い選択条項
option holder
オプション保有者
oral contract
口頭による契約、口約束
orange goods
オレンジ商品
or better
〔株式〕指値かまたはそれ以上で
order
注文、受注（為替・手形の）受注高、指図

order bill of lading
指図式船荷証券
order card
注文カード、
作業指図書
order entry
注文入力、受注、
オーダーエントリー
order flow pattern
受注（注文）の流れパターン、
受注フローパターン
order form
注文書式、注文用紙
order number
注文番号
order paper
注文書類、注文控え帳
order-point system
発注点方式
order regulation
注文の規則
ordinal scale
順序尺度
ordinance
法令、布告、命令
ordinary and necessary business expense
通常必要な営業費
ordinary annuity
普通年金
ordinary course of business
普通の業務過程
ordinary gain or ordinary income
経常収入、経常利益、
通常所得
ordinary interest
通常利息、通常利子、
通常金利
ordinary loss
経常損失
ordinary payroll exclusion endorsement
通常給料除外指示
organization
組織、機構、協会
organizational behavior
組織行動
organizational chart
組織図、会社構成図
organization cost
創業費
organization development
組織開発
organization planning
組織計画
organization structure
組織構造
organized labor
組織労働
orientation
オリエンテーション、
（新入社員などの）指導、
方向付け
original cost
取得原価、
仕入原価
original entry
初記入、原始記入
original issue discount (OID)
発売時割引

original maturity
オリジナルマチュリティ、当初満期
original order
最初の注文
origination fee
融資開始手数料、融資取組み手数料
originator
創作者、創始者、原資産所有者
other income
雑所得、雑益、営業外所得
other insurance clause
他保険条項
other people's money
借入金
outbid
高値をつける、せりに勝つ
outcry market
競売市場
out of the money
アウトオブザマネー
outlet store
アウトレット店、販売店、在庫処分店、直売店
outline view
概観図
outside director
外部重役、社外重役、社外取締役
outsourcing
外部調達、外注、外部委託
outstanding
未決済の、未払いの、（pl.）未払い負債
outstanding balance
未済残高、未払残高、融資残高
outstanding capital stock
株式発行高、資本金現在高
overage
規定年齢を超えた、適齢を過ぎた、過多量
overall expenses method
総費用方式
overall rate of return
総収益率
over-and-short
過不足の
overbooked
超過予約である、オーバーブックッキング
overbought
過剰買いの
overcharge
不当な値段、不当な要求、
overflow
過多、過剰、オーバーフロー
overhang
張り出す、突き出る、余剰の
overhead
諸掛込みの、諸経費、間接費
overheating
（景気の）過熱
overimprovement
過剰改良
overissue
（通貨、証券の）

過大発行
overkill
やり過ぎ、行き過ぎ、オーバーキル
overpayment
払い過ぎ、支払超過
overproduction
生産過剰、過剰生産
override
無視する、無効にする、（売上・利益に応じた）コミッション、歩合
overrun
（予算、見積もりを）超過する、見積もり超過額、過剰支出額
over (short)
~以上、~より多く（~以下、～より少なく）
over the counter (OTC)
（株券、証券などが）（取引所を通さずに）直接売買された、店頭売買
over-the-counter retailing
店頭小売り
overtime
残業時間、超過勤務時間、残業手当
overtrading
資金超過取引
overvalued
過大評価の
owner-operator
自営業者
ownership
所有権
ownership form
所有形態

P

pacesetter
(仕事の)進度設定者
package
荷造り、一括、小包
package band
パッケージバンド
package code
パッケージコード
package design
パッケージデザイン、
包装デザイン
packaged goods
包装品
package mortgage
包括抵当
packing list
荷造目録、包装明細書
padding
詰め物用の材料、詰め物、
（帳簿上の）不正な経費
page break
改ページ、ページの区切り
page down
次のページへ
page format
ページ形式
page up
前のページへ
pagination
枚数、丁付け、ページ付け
paid in advance
前払いした
paid in capital
払込資金
paid-in surplus
払込剰余金
paid status
支払済み状態、
支払済みステータス
paintbrush
絵筆、ペンキ用のはけ、
ペントブラシュ
painting the tape
証券偽装取引
palmtop
パームトップ、
手の平に載せて使える小型の
paper
手形、紙幣、（pl.）書類
paper jam
紙詰まり
paper gold
ペーパー・ゴールド
（IMF の特別引出権）
paper money
紙幣
paper profit (loss)
紙上利益（損失）、
架空利益（損失）、
見込利益（損失）

par
額面価格、平価、為替平価
paralegal
弁護士補助員
parallel processing
並列処理、並行処理、パラレルプロセシング
parameter
パラメーター、媒介変数、補助変数
par bond
額面売買債券、額面価格債券
parallel connection
パラレル接続、並列接続
parcel
一口の取引、一組、～を分配する
parent company
親会社
parity
（品質、等級、価格などの）同等、平衡価格、等価
parity check
パリティチェック、奇遇検査
parity price
パリティ価格、平価
parking
駐車場
parliamentary procedure
議会手続き
partial delivery
一部受渡し、分割出荷
partial equilibrium analysis
部分均衡分析
partial release
抵当一部解除、段階的解除
partial taking
土地の一部収用
participating insurance
利益配当付き保険
participating policy
利益配当付き保険証書
participating preferred stock
参加優先株式
participation certificate
参加証書
participation loan
協調融資、参加貸付け
participative budgeting
参加型予算編成
participative leadership
参加型指導者、参加型指導（統率、指揮）
partition
分割、部分、仕切り
partner
仲間、共同出資者、パートナー
partnership
共同、協力、共同経営
part-time
パートタイムの、非常勤の
par value
為替平価、額面価額
passed dividend
（未払いの）保留配当、見送り配当、無配
passenger mile
旅客マイル

passive activities
受動的活動
passive income (loss)
受動的所得（損失）
passive investor
受動的投資家
passport
旅券、パスポート、
（比喩的に）保障
pass-through security
パススルー証券
password
パスワード、合い言葉、
暗証番号
paste
貼り付ける、ペースト
past service benefit
過去勤務給付、
過去勤務年金
patent
特許、特許権、
土地譲渡証書
patent infringement
特許権侵害
patent monopoly
特許権独占、専売特許
patent of invention
発明特許
patent pending
特許出願中
patent warfare
特許争い
paternalism
父権主義、父権的干渉
（統制）、パターナリズム
path
パス、経路
patronage dividend and rebate
利益配当および割引
(払戻し、リベート、
割戻し）
pauper
救貧法受給者
pay
支給、給料、支払う
payables
支払債務、買入債務、掛金
pay as you go
現金支払主義
payback period
返済期間、資本回収期間、
払戻期間
paycheck
給料、俸給、給与
payday
給料日、俸給日、
支払日
payee
被支払人、受取人
payer
支払人、払渡人
paying agent
支払代理人
payload
給金負担高、有料荷重
payment bond
支払保証、返還保証証券、
払込み債
payment date
支払期日

payment in due course
満期払い
payment method
支払方法、料金設定、
返済方法
payola
リベート、
賄賂
payout
支払（金）、（投資の）回収、配当（金）、
元金回収
payout ratio
配当性向、
配当支払率
pay period
給与期間
payroll
給与、給料、支払台帳、賃金支払帳、給与者名簿
payroll deduction
賃金控除
payroll savings plan
給料天引き貯金プラン
payroll tax
給与税、賃金税
peak
景気の山
peak period
最高期間、ピーク時
peculation
公金横領、受託金横領者
pecuniary
金銭（上）の、財政
（上）の、罰金を課せるべき
peg
釘付けにする、（株の売買によって高騰・低落を）
安定させる、
(為替相場の騰落を）抑える
penalty
罰金、違約金
penny stock
ペニー株、投機的低位株、
投機的安物株
pension fund
年金基金、恩給基金
peon
日雇い人、日雇い労働者
people intensive
人手集約的な
per capita
一人当たり、頭割りで
per-capita debt
一人当たりの負債
percentage lease
歩合制リース、
歩合制賃貸借率
percentage-of-completion method
工事進行比率法、
工事進行基準法
percentage-of-sales method
売上比率法
percent, percentage
パーセント、百分率
percolation test
浸透試験
per diem
毎日当り、
１日当り

perfect competition
完全競争
perfect (pure) monopoly
完全独占
（＝ABSOLUTE MONOPOLY）
perfected
大成された、完成された
performance
遂行、履行、成績、業績
performance bond
契約履行保証,
契約保証保険
performance fund
パフォーマンスファンド
performance stock
業績株
period
期間
period expense, period cost
期間費用、期間原価
periodic inventory method
定期的棚卸法
peripheral device
周辺機器、周辺装置
perishable perjury
消滅しやすい偽証罪
permanent difference
永久差異
permanent financing
永久貸出し、
永久的資金調達
permit
許す、許可、許可証
permit bond
保証を許可する
permutations
順列、置換、並べ換え
perpetual inventory
継続棚卸、恒久的棚卸
perpetuity
永続、終身年金、永久所有
perquisite (perk)
（定収入、給料、
賃金以外の）付加給与、
特別給付
person
人、自然人、人間、個人
personal data sheet
個人データ表
personal digital assistant (PDA)
パーソナルデジタル
アシスタント、
携帯情報端末
personal financial statement
個人の財産状況報告書
personal holding company (PHC)
個人持ち株会社
personal income
個人所得
personal influence
パーソナルインフルエンス、
個人的影響
personal injury
人身傷害、人体損傷、
個人的権利に対する被害
personal liability
人的責任、個人的責任、
個人的負債

personal property
人的財産（権）、動産、
個人財産
personal property floater
動産包括保険、
動産包括保険証券
personal selling
対個人販売、人的販売、
personnel
職員、人員、人材
personnel department
（会社の）人事課
petition
請願（書）、陳情（書）、
申請する
petty cash fund
小口現金、
小払い用現金
Phillip's curve
フィリップス曲線
physical commodity
実物商品
physical depreciation
物質的減価、物量的減価、
物理的減価
physical examination
身体検査、健康診断
physical inventory
現物棚卸、実地棚卸、
実在庫量
picketing
ピケを張る
picture format
ピクチャフォーマット、
ピクチャ形式
piece rate
単価、出来高払い、
請負単価
piece work
出来高（払いの）仕事、
請負仕事、賃仕事
pie chart
円グラフ、円分グラフ、
パイ図表
pier to house
埠頭（桟橋）から戸口へ
piggyback loan
ピギーバックローン
pilot plan
パイロットプラン、
実験的計画、試験的計画
pin money
小額の金、はした金
pipeline
パイプライン、輸送管路、
流通経路
pitch
ピッチ、
（文字、行などの）送り
pixel/picture element
ピクセル、画素
pixel image
ピクセルイメージ、
ピクセル画像
placement test
就職試験、
従業員の採用試験、
（人員）配置テスト
place utility
場所効果

plain text
普通テキスト
plaintiff
訴訟人、原告、起訴人
plan
(物事を進める）計画、案、制度（年金などの必要資金の）
plan B
計画Ｂ
planned economy
計画的経済
plant
植物、作物、施設
plat
小さな地面（地所）、図面
plat book
プラットブック、
地所台帳、土地登録簿
pleading
訴答、訴訟手続き、申立書
pledge
誓約、担保
plot
陰謀、計画、構想
plot plan
配置図、敷地計画図、プロットプラン
plottage value
敷地価値、合筆価額
plotter
陰謀者、
地図（図面）
製作者
plow back
（資本などを）
再投資する
plus tick
景気の上昇、
前回より高い出来値
pocket computer
ポケットコンピューター
point
［商業］刻み、ポイント
point chart
点図表、ポイントチャート
poison pill
［金融］
ポイズンピル防衛戦略
Poisson distribution
ポワソン分布
police power
警察権、治安（維持）
権
policy holder
保険契約者
policy loan
保険証券貸付、契約者貸付
pollution
汚染、汚すこと
pool
企業連合、
割り当てカルテル、
プール
pooling of interests
持分プーリング法
portal-to-portal
pay
拘束時間賃金
portfolio
ポートフォリオ
（各種の金融資産の集合）

有価証券明細書
portfolio beta score
ポートフォリオのベータスコア
portfolio income
ポートフォリオの収入
portfolio manager
ポートフォリオマネジャー、資産管理担当者
portfolio reinsurance
ポートフォリオ再保険
portfolio theory
ポートフォリオ理論
port of entry
輸入港、手続港、通関港
portrait (format)
横向き（形式）
position
位置、適所、為替持高
positioning
位置付け、位置決め
positive confirmation
積極的確認
positive leverage
正のレバレッジ
positive yield curve
正の利回り曲線
possession
所有、占有、所有物
post closing trial balance
締切り後試算表、繰越試算表
posting
記帳、転記
posting (computer)
転記すること、記入する
poverty
貧乏
power connection
電源接続
power down
電源を切る、パワーをさげる、出力をさげる
power of attorney
委任状、委任権（委任状にもとづく）代理権
power of sale
売却権
power surge
サージ電圧、サージ電流
power up
電源を入れる、パワーを上げる、出力をあげる
practical capacity
実際的生産能力、実用容量、実用生産能力
pre-bill
予備請求、前もって請求する
precautionary motive
警戒的動機、事前対応的動機
preclosing
締め切り前の
precompute
あらかじめ演算する
prediction
予測、予報
preemptive rights
（優先的）新株引受権、

先買い権
preexisting use
すでに存在している使用
prefabricated
前もって作り上られた（製造された）、作成済みの、プレハブの
preferential rehiring
優先的再雇用
preferred dividend
優先配当
preferred dividend coverage
優先配当適用率
preferred stock
優先株
prelease
建築開始以前に結ぶ賃貸借契約、
賃貸借契約を建築前に結ぶ
preliminary prospectus
予備設立趣意書、
仮目論見書
premises
（建物を含めた）土地、
〔法律〕（理由付けの）
前提
premium
割増し価格、保険料、
手数料
premium bond
割増金付き債権
premium income
保険料収入
premium pay
奨励給、奨励給与
premium rate
保険料率
prenuptial agreement
結婚前の同意契約
prepaid
前払いした
prepaid expense
前払経費
prepaid-interest
前払利息
prepayment
満期前支払い、中途償還、
前払金
prepayment clause
中途償還条項、
前払金条項
prepayment penalty
前払い罰則手数料
prepayment privilege
前払い特典（特権）
prerogative
(地位、職務に与えられる）
特権、特典
presale
プレセール、
セール前特別セール
prescription
命令（指示、規定）
すること、〔法律〕
（取得）時効
presentation
プレゼンテーション、
提出、提示
present fairly
…を正しく示す、
…を公平に提示する

present value
現在価値、現在価格、
現在価額
present value of 1
１の現価
present value of annuity
年金の現在価値、
年金現価
president
社長、会長、総裁、長官、
頭取、級長
presold issue
事前売却済公債発行
press kit
記者会見時に配る資料一式、
宣伝資料
prestige advertising
評判の高い広告、
有名な広告、立派な広告
prestige pricing
名声価格
pretax earnings
課税前の収入、税込所得
pretax rate of return
税込み収益率、
税引き前収益率
preventive maintenance
予防保全、予防保守、
予防整備
price elasticity
価格弾力性
price-fixing
価格の固定、価格協定
price index
物価指数、価格指数
price lining
価格ライン
price stabilization
価格安定、価格安定化
price support
価格支持、価格維持
price system
価格制度、価格体制
price war
価格戦、値引き競争
pricey
高価な、値段の高い
pricing below market
市場価格以下の値付け
primary boycott
一次的ボイコット
primary demand
第一次需要、基本的需要
primary distribution
第一次分売
primary earnings per (common) share
１株当りの本源的収益
primary lease
第一次賃借権、
第一次リース
primary market
主要市場、
一次市場
primary market area
主要市場地域、
一次市場地域
primary package
プライマリーパッケージ

prime paper
優良手形、一流手形

prime rate
プライムレート、
最優遇貸出金利

prime tenant
主要賃借人

principal
主な、主要な、元金

principal amount
元金、元本金額

principal and interest payment (p&i)
元利払い

principal, interest, taxes, and insurance payment (PITI)
元利税金および保険料払い

principal residence
主たる住居（住所）

principal stock holder
主要株主

principal sum
元金、（保険契約に基づいた）支払金

printer
プリンター、印刷機

printout
プリントアウト、印刷、プリンターで印刷されたもの

prior period adjustment
前期損益修正、
過年度損益修正

prior-preferred stock
前期優先株

prior service cost
事前業務コスト、過去勤務費用、過去勤務債務

privacy laws
プライバシー法、
私生活の権利に関係する法

private cost
私的費用

private limited partnership
私的有限責任合資会社、
小さな合資会社

private mortgage insurance
民間抵当保険、
自家抵当保険

private offering or private placement
（債券などの）私募、プライベートプレースメント、
私募発行、第三者割当て

privatization
民営化

privity
〔法律〕当事者間の関係

prize broker
第一級のブローカー、
一流ブローカー

probate
（遺言の）検認をする、
検認済みの遺言書、保護観察に付す

probationary employee
試用従業員、見習い従業員

proceeds
収入、売上金、売上高

proceeds from resale
再販の売上高

processor upgrade
処理装置（プロセサー）の品質改良
procurement
調達、獲得、買い上げ
procuring cause
購買成立原因（住宅などの売買成立の結果をもたらした原因となった人）
produce
生み出す、作り出す、製造する
producer cooperative
生産者協同組合、製作者協同組合
producer goods
生産財（消費財の生産を助ける財、機械、原料品など）
product
生産物、生産品、製品
production
生産、産出、製造、製作
production control
生産管理、工程管理
production-oriented organization
生産志向組織（機構、体制）
production-possibility curve
生産可能性曲線
production rate
生産率
production worker
生産労働者
productivity
生産性、生産力
product liability
製造物責任
product liability insurance
製造物責任保険
product life cycle
製品寿命、プロダクトライフサイクル
product line
プロダクトライン、製品種目
product mix
複合生産物、製品組合せ
profession
職業（特に知的職業）、公言、（集合的）同業者仲間
profit
利益、収益、利潤
profitability
収益性、利潤性
profit and loss statement (p&l)
損益計算書
profit center
プロフィットセンター、利益中心点、利益責任単位
profiteer
不当利得者、暴利商人、暴利を貪る
profit margin
利鞘、利潤差額、利益率
profit motive
利潤動機、営利主義

profit and commissions form
利益・手数料書式
profit-sharing plan
利益分配制度
profit squeeze
利潤圧縮
profit system
利潤制度
profit taking
利食い、利潤獲得
program budgeting
プログラム予算を計上する
programmer
プログラム作成者、
プログラマー
programming language
プログラミング言語
program trade
プログラム売買
progressive tax
累進税
progress payments
分割払い
projected benefit obligation
予測給付債務
projected (proforma) financial statement
見積財務諸表
projection
予測、見積り、投出
promissory note
約束手形
promotional allowance
促進割引、販売促進引当金
promotion mix
プロモーションミックス
proof of loss
損害証明、損失証明
property
財産、所有物、所有権
property line
土地の境界線
property management
財産管理、不動産管理
property report
財産報告
property rights
財産権
property tax
財産税、固定資産税、
不動産税
proprietary interest
所有権、持分、
独占的所有権
proprietary lease
所有者賃貸借契約
proprietorship
所有主持分、個人企業、
正味財産
prorate
〜を比例配分する
prospect
見込み、公算、展望
prospective rating
予想料率算定
prospectus
創立趣意書、
目論見書
protected file
保護ファイル

protectionism
保護貿易主義、
保護政策
protocol
条約原案、条約議定書、
（国家間の）補足協約
proviso
但し書き、条件
proxy
代理、代理権、代理人
proxy fight
代理戦争、
委任状投票決戦
proxy statement
委任状
prudence
賢明さ、慎重
psychic income
心理的収入
public accounting
公認会計士会計報告、
公会計
public domain
公有、社会の共有財産、公
物
public employee
公務員
public held
公共所有の
public record
公文書、公記録
public relations (pr)
広報、宣伝活動、
ピーアール
public sale
公開売却
public use
公用
public works
公共（土木）工事、
公共事業
puffing
値を競り上げること
pump priming
景気刺激、景気刺激策、
経済振興策
（公共投資による）
punch list
未決済事項の表
punitive damages
懲罰的損害賠償
purchase
購入、買入れ、買いけつ
purchase journal
仕入帳、仕入仕訳帳
purchase money mortgage
購入代金抵当
purchase order
買付注文、購入注文
purchasing power
購買力
pure capitalism
純粋資本主義
pure competition
純粋競争
pure-market economy
純粋市場経済
push money (PM)
特別報奨金
put option
解消（売り・延期）選択権、
プットオプション
put to seller
「プット・ツー・セラー」
〔プットオプションを行使
するさいに使われる表現〕

pyramiding
株式の買（売）乗せ、利乗せすること、漸増すること

p **value**
p 価値

Q

qualified endorsement
限定裏書
qualified opinion
限定意見
qualified plan or qualified trust
受給資格制度（あるいは信託）
qualified terminable interest property (Q-TIP) trust
受給資格期限付利子財産信託
qualitative analysis
定性分析
qualitative research
定性調査
quality
品質、質
quality control
品質管理
quality engineering
品質工学
quantitative analysis
定量分析、量的分析
quantitative research
定量調査、数量調査
quantity discount
数量割引
quarterly
毎期の、年４回の、四半期の、季刊誌
quasi contract
準契約
query
問合せ、照会、照会文
queue
待ち行列、キュー
quick asset
当座資産
quick ratio
当座比率
quiet enjoyment
平穏享有権
quiet title suit
権原確認訴訟、土地所有権保全訴訟
quitclaim deed
権利放棄型捺印証書、無担保譲渡証書
quorum
定足数、（合議などの）必要員数
quota
一定割合、割当数、枠
quota sample
割当標本

quotation
相場、時価、見積

quo warranto
権限開示令状

qwerty keyboard
クワーテイキーボード

qwertz keyboard
クワーズキーボード

R

racket
不正な金儲け、密売
rag content
ぼろ含有量
raider
（株買占めで会社を）
乗っ取る人、不正摘発者
rain insurance
雨害保険
raised check
変造小切手
rally
盛り返し、回復する
random access memory (RAM)
ランダムアクセス記憶装置、ランダムアクセスメモリー、RAM
random-digit dialing
ランダムディジタルダイヤリング
random-number generator
乱数発生器
random sample
ランダムサンプル、
任意抽出見本
random walk
〔統計〕乱歩、（経済）千鳥足（理論）、
ランダムウォーク（法）
range
範囲、区域、限界
rank-and file
一般人、一般庶民、
一般社員
ratable
評価しうる、
（英）課税しうる
rate
割合、歩合、評価する
rate base
料金算定基準
rate card
料金表
rated policy
評定保険証券
rates and classifications
料率と等級
rate setting
賃率設定
ratification
承認、認可、批准
rating
格付け、評価、採点
ratio analysis
比率分析
rationing
配給（の）

ratio scale
比例尺度
raw data
生データ
raw land
未開発地
raw material
原料
reading the tape
テープ読み取り
readjustment
再調整、財政建て直し
read-only
読取り専用
real
本当の、実在する、実際の
real account
実在勘定、実体勘定
real earnings
実質所得、実質収入
real estate
不動産
real estate investment trust (REIT)
不動産投資信託
real estate market
不動産市場
real estate owned (REO)
所有されている不動産
real income
実質所得
real interest rate
実質利子率、実質金利
realized gain
実現収益
real property
不動産、物的財産
real rate of return
実勢利益率
realtor
公認不動産業者〔商標〕
real value of money
貨幣の実質価値
real wages
実質賃金
reappraisal lease
再評価リース
reasonable person
道理をわきまえた人
reassessment
再評価、再検討
rebate
割戻し、払い戻し、
リベート
reboot
リブート、再起動、
リブートする
recall
リコール、
（欠陥商品などの）
回収、撤回
recall campaign
回収キャンペーン
recall study
リコール研究
recapitalization
資本修正、資本再編成
recapture
再捕獲、
再収集

recapture rate
再捕獲率
recasting a debt
負債を再計算すること
receipt, receipt book
受取り、領収証、受取証、受取台帳
receivables turnover
受取勘定回転率
receiver
受取人、領収者、会計係
receiver's certificate
管財人証明書
receivership
管財人の役職
receiving clerk
受取係、収入係
receiving record
受取記録、領収記録
recession
景気後退、不景気、リセッション
reciprocal buying
相互購買
reciprocity
互恵主義、相互利益、交換再保険
reckoning
計算、集計、勘定
recognition
認可、承認、表彰
recognized gain
認識利益
recompense
賠償、償い、補償
reconciliation
和解、調停、調和
reconditioning property
財産の修理
reconsign
～を再委託する
reconveyance
再譲渡、前所有者に返還
record
記録、登記、登録
recorder point
レコーダーポイント
recording
記録、記載
records management
記録情報管理
recoup, recoupment
損害を回復する、（損失を）取り戻す、弁償する、賠償、控除
recourse
（手形・小切手などの）遡及（権）、償還請求（権）、償還
recourse loan
リコースローン、償還準備貸付（金）
recover
回復する、取り戻す
recovery
改修、回復
recovery fund
回復資金
recovery of basis
基準の回復

recruitment
採用、補充、募集
recruitment bonus
採用ボーナス
recycle bin
ごみ箱
recycling
再生利用、再循環
redeem
買戻す、質受けする、
償還する
redemption
買戻し、償還、償却
redemption period
償還期間、買戻し期間
redevelop
再開発する
rediscount
再割引する、再割引
rediscount rate
再割引率、再割引利率
redlining
（銀行・保険会社による）
特別警戒地区指定、融資・
保険契約指し止め地区指定
red tape
官僚的形式主義、繁文縟礼
reduced rate
割引料金
reduction certificate
値引保証書
referee
仲裁人、裁決者、審判員
referral
参照、照会
refinance
財政を立て直す、資金を補
充する、リファイナンス
reformation
再構成、改良
refresh
リフレッシュする、
復元する、再生する
refunding
（金）の返済、償還、
払戻し
refund
返済する、払い戻す、
返済
registered bond
記名式債券、登録式債券
registered check
登録小切手
registered company
登録会社
registered investment company
登録投資会社
registered representative
（株式取引所の会員証券会
社の従業員である）
登録代理人
registered security
記名証券
registrar
登記係、公認の記録係、
株式名簿係
registration
記録、登録、
登記

registration statement
登録届出書
registry of deeds
捺印証書の登録（登記）、権利書の登記
regression analysis
回帰分析
regression line
回帰直線
regressive tax
累退税
regular-way delivery (and settlement)
通常受渡し（および決済、清算）
regulated commodities
統制商品
regulated industry
統制された産業、統制産業
regulated investment company
統制投資会社
regulation
調整、調節、規則
regulatory agency
監督官庁、規制機関
rehabilitation
更生、再建、復興
reindustrialization
再工業化
reinstatement
復権、回復、契約復活
reinsurance
再保険
reinvestment privilege
再投資特権
reinvestment rate
再投資収益率
related party transaction
関連当事者取引
release
開放、解除、放免、譲渡
release clause
免除条項、解除条項、譲渡条項
relevance
（当面する問題どの）関連性
reliability
信頼性
relocate
移転する（させる）
remainder
残り、残り物
remainderman
残余権者
remedy
救済方法、賠償、弁償
remit
支払う、罪などを免除する、軽減する
remit rate
支払い率
remonetization
再び通貨とすること
remote access
遠隔アクセス、リモートアクセスする
remuneration
給料、報酬、報償

renegotiate
再交渉する
renegotiated rate mortgage (RRM)
再調整金利モーゲージ
renewable natural resource
再生可能天然資源
renewal option
更新選択権、更新選択肢
rent
家賃、賃借（賃貸）する
rentable area
賃貸可能面積
rental rate
賃貸料、レンタル料、賃料率
rent control
家賃統制、地代家賃統制
rent-free period
家賃無料期間
rent-up period
レントアップ期間
reopener clause
（契約条項の）交渉再開条項
reorganization
再組織、再編成、〔金融〕再建
repairs
修繕作業
repatriation
（手形などの）再提出、再提示
replace
置換する、置き換わる、更新
replacement cost
再取得価格、取替費用
replacement cost accounting
取替原価会計
replacement reserve
補充引当金、設備更新準備金
replevin
動産占有回復訴訟
reporting currency
報告通貨
repressive tax
抑制的課税
reproduction cost
再生産費、再生産費用、（機械設備などの）再取得原価
repudiation
拒否、債務履行の拒否、国債（公債）の支払拒否
repurchase agreement (repo; rp)
買戻し約定
reputation
評判
request for proposal (RFP)
見積依頼（書）、提案依頼（書）
required rate of return
必要収益率、最低所要利益率

requisition
請求、請求（書）、
注文（書）
release proceeds
譲渡収入、公開収入
rescission
無効にすること、
契約解除、
計上予算撤回
research
研究（する）、調査（す
る）
research and development (R&D)
研究開発
research department
研究部門
research intensive
研究集約的
reserve
保存、予備（品）、準備金
reserve fund
積立金
reserve requirement
準備預金規定
reserve-stock control
予約株式統制
reset
リセットする、
規定値にもどす
resident buyer
駐在仕入人
resident buying office
駐在仕入事務所
residential
住宅の、居住の
residential broker
住宅ブローカー、
住宅仲介業者
residential district
住宅区域、住宅地域
residential credit
住宅信用貸し
residential energy credit
住宅エネルギー貸付け
（融資）
residential service contract
住宅サービス契約
residual value
残存価値、残存価額
resolution
決議
respondent
応答する人、回答者、被告
（特に離婚訴訟の）
response
応答、回答
response projection
応答の予測、回答見積
restart
再始動する（させる）、
再起動する（
させる）
restitution
（損害の）賠償、補償、
回復
restraint of trade
取引の制限
restraint of alienation
譲渡制限
restricted surplus
制限付き余剰金

restriction
規制、限定、制限
restrictive covenant
制限契約
retail
小売
retail credit
小売信用
retail display allowance
小売陳列割引
retailer's service program
小売サービスプログラム
retail inventory method
小売棚卸し法
retail outlet
小売販売店
retail rate
小売レート
retaining
保有（保持）すること、損続させること、（弁護しなどを）雇っておくこと
retained earnings
利益積立金、任意積立金、社内保留利益金
retained earnings, appropriated
処分済み保留利益
retained earnings statement
保留利益計算書
retaliatory eviction
報復的追立て
retire
退く、退職する、廃物にする
retirement
退職、年金、（債券などの）回収・満期償還
retirement age
退職年齢
retirement fund
退職基金、退職資金
retirement income
退職所得
retirement plan
退職金制度
retroactive
遡及する、（過去のある時期に）さかのぼって、逆戻りの
retroactive adjustment
遡及調整
return
収益、返品、返却する
return on capital
資本収益、資本利益
return on equity
株式資本利益
return on invested capital
投資資本利益
return on pension plan assets
年金計画資産利益
return on sales
売上利益
returns
総売上高、利回り、収益
revaluation
平価切上げ、再評価

revenue
（国家の）歳入、収益、
収入
revenue anticipation
note
(RAN)
収入予想証券

revenue bond
収益担保債、
歳入担保債、
特定財源債
revenue ruling
内国歳入規則
reversal
反転、逆転、転換
reverse annuity mortgage
(RAM)
（年齢方式）逆住宅ローン
reverse leverage
逆梃率、負の梃率効果
reverse split
逆分割
reversing entry
逆記入
reversion
復帰権、財産復帰
reversionary factor
復帰権的要因、
復帰権的ファクター
reversionary interest
復帰権的権利
reversionary value
復帰権的価値
review
批評、再考、再検討、審査
revocable trust
撤回可能信託、
取消可能信託
revocation
撤回、取消、破棄
revolving charge
account
回転売掛金勘定
revolving credit
回転信用、回転信用状
revolving fund
回転基金、回転資金、リヴ
ォルビング基金
rezoning
再区分（の）、区分変更
（の）
rich
金持ちの、富んだ、豊富な
rich text format (RTF)
リッチテキストフォーマッ
ト、RTF フォーマット
rider
添書き、追加条項、
付加条項
right of first refusal
最優先引受権行使の拒絶、
第一先買権行使の拒絶
right of redemption
買戻し権、取戻し権
right of rescission
解約権、撤回
right of return
返却権、帰還権、
買戻し請求権
right of survivorship
生存者権、残存者取得権

right-of-way
先行権、優先通行権、
通行権
risk
リスク、危険、危険負担
risk-adjusted discount rate
危険調整割引率
risk arbitrage
リスクアービトラージ、
危険鞘取り売買
risk averse
リスク回避的な
risk management
リスクマネジメント、
危機管理
rolling stock
（鉄道の）車両、
貨物自動車
rollover
回転、乗り換え、借り換え
rollover loan
回転貸付、
ロールオーバーローン
ROM (read-only memory)
ROM、ロム、読出し専用
メモリー
rotating shift
交替制、輪番
roundhouse
転写台付き機関車、
（後甲板の）後部船室
round lot
最低取引単位、
まとまった株数
royalty
ロイヤルティ、使用料、
許諾料、印税
royalty trust
使用料信託
run
経営する、（契約などを）
継続する、有効である
rundown
（情報などの）要約、
まとめ、〔証券〕最終値相
場表要約
run of paper (ROP)
（新聞・雑誌の広告の）
掲載位置編集者一任
run with the land
土地とともに移転する
rural
田舎の
rurban
田園都市の

S

sabotage
サボタージュ、妨害（する）、破壊（する）
safe harbor rule
安全港ルール、承認領域ルール、安全ルール
safekeeping
保管
safety commission
安全手数料
safety margin
安全マージン
salariat
俸給生活者階級、
サラリーマン
salary
俸給、給料、月給
salary reduction plan
俸給減少計画
sale
販売、売却、
売渡し
sale and leaseback
リース契約付き売却
sale or exchange
売却あるいは交換
sales analyst
売上分析者
sales budget
販売予算
sales charge
売費用
sales contract
販売契約
sales effectiveness test
販売効果テスト
sales incentive
売上奨励手当
sales journal
売上仕訳帳、売上帳
sales letter
売込み状
salesperson
販売店員、売り子
sales portfolio
売上高明細表
sales promotion
販売促進
sales returns and allowances
返品調整引当金
sales revenue
売上収益、総売上高
sales tax
（英）物品税、
（米）物品販売税、
売上税
sales type lease
販売型リース

salvage value
救出財貨価格
（売却金）
sample buyer
見本購入者
sampling
サンプリング、見本抽出、
抜取り
sandwich lease
（不動産）原貸借、
サンドイッチリース
satellite communication
衛星通信
satisfaction of a debt
負債の償還、負債の弁済、
負債の弁済証書
satisfaction piece
債務履行証書、返済証書
savings bond
貯蓄債券、貯蓄公債
savings element
(生命保険の)貯蓄要素
savings rate
貯蓄率
scab
労働組合非加入者、
スト破り
scalage
（縮み、漏れなどの恐れのある品物の値段の）差引率
scale
目盛、尺度、指数、等級
scale (computer)
位取り、目盛、物差し
scale order
刻み注文
scale relationship
関係（係わり合い、
結びつき、取引先など）
を天秤にかける
scalper
株券を素早く売買してわずかな利鞘を稼ぐ人、ダフ屋
scanner
スキャナー、走査器
scarcity, scarcity value
欠乏、不足；稀少価値
scatter diagram
散布図
scatter plan
散布図面
scenic easement
景観地役権
schedule
一覧表、時間表、予定、
予定する、表をつくる
scheduling
日程計画
scheduled production
計画された生産品
（高、額）
scienter
故意に
scope of employment
雇用範囲
scorched-earth
defense
焦土防御（策）
screen filter
スクリーンフィルター
screen saver
スクリーンセーバー

scrip
仮株券、仮証券、
仮債券
scroll down
スクロールダウン
scroll up
スクロールアップ
seal
印、封印、印章、印証、
確証（保証、契約）
のしるし
sealed bid
封緘入札
seal of approval
承認の印章
search engine
サーチエンジン、
検索エンジン
seasonal adjustment
季節調整
seasonality
季節性
seasoned issue
確実証券
seasoned loan
堅実融資
seat
所在地、（証券取引所などの）会員券、議席、役職
secondary boycott
第二次ボイコット
secondary distribution
(既発行証券の)
第二次分売
secondary market
流通市場、第二次市場
secondary mortgage market
第二次抵当市場
second lien or second mortgage
二番抵当、第二順位抵当
second mortgage lending
二番抵当貸付
second-preferred stock
低位優先株
sector
部門、産業部門、セクター
secured bond
担保付き社債、
担保付き債券
secured debt
担保付き負債
secured transaction
担保付き取引
securities
証券、有価証券
securities analyst
証券分析家、
証券アナリスト
securities and commodities exchanges
証券商品取引所
Securities and Exchange Commission (SEC)
〔米〕証券取引委員会
securities loan
証券担保貸出し、証券金融、
証券貸付け
security
保証、担保、
（通常 pl.）
有価証券

security deposit
敷金
security interest
〔法律〕先取特権、担保権
security rating
担保評価・格付け
seed money
（新事業の）元手、
着手資金、投機的資金
segmentation strategy
分割戦略、市場分断戦略
segment margin
事業区分別利ざや、
セグメントマージン
segment reporting
事業区分別損益報告、セグメントリポート
segregation of duties
任務の分割化、
関税の区分化
seisin
（土地の）占有（権）、
所有（権）
select
選択する、選択
selective credit control
選択的信用統制、選択的信用調整
selective distribution
選択的販売経路、
選択的販売
self-amortizing mortgage
自己償還的抵当貸付
self-directed IRA
自己決定個人退職積立勘定（IRA）
self employed
自営業の、自営業者の
self-help
自助、自助努力、
セルフヘルプ

self insurance
自家保険、自己保険
self-tender offer
自己株式公開買付け制度
seller's market
売手市場
sell-in
売り込む
selling agent or selling broker
販売代理店、販売仲買人
selling climax
セリングクライマックス
selling short
空売り
sell-off
売崩し
semiannual
半年の、半期の、
半年ごとの
semiconductor
セミコンダクター、半導体
semimonthly
月二回の、半月ごと
semivariable costs
半変動費
senior debt
優位弁済債務、上位債務
senior refunding
優位（上位、優先）償還、

優位（上位、優先）払戻し
senior security
優位（上位、優先）担保（保証、抵当、証券（*pl*）
sensitive market
不安定市場
sensitivity training
グループ研究、
人間関係セミナー
sentiment indicators
センチメント指標
separate property
特有財産
serial bond
連続償還債券
serial port
シリアルポート
series bond
連続発行債券
server
サーバー
service
役務、客扱い、サービス業
service bureau
サービスビューロ、サービス機関
service club
奉仕クラブ、福祉団体
service department
サービス部門、サービス係
service economy
サービス経済、奉仕経済
service fee
手数料、サービス料金
service worker
サービス業労働者、
～業従事者
servicing
供給、サービス
setback
頓挫、セットバック
setoff
債務の差引、（損失等の）
埋め合わせ、相殺する
settle
清算する、決算する、
安定させる
settlement
解決、支払い、清算
settlement date
決算日、決済日、勘定日
settlor
設定者、財産譲渡者
severalty
（財産の）単独保有、
単独土地保有
severance damages
残地損失
severance pay
解雇手当、退職金
sexual harassment
性的嫌がらせ、
セクハラ
shakedown
強奪、ゆすり、徹底的捜索
shakeout
淘汰、（株などの）暴落、
小投資家の淘汰、組織の合理化・刷新
shakeup
（人事・組織の）大整理、
再編成

share
割当て、分担、共有権、
株式、共有する、
分配する
sharecropper
シェアクロッパー、
分益小作人
shared-appreciation mortgage (SAM)
抵当物件増加分共有条件貸付け、
SAM 方式抵当貸付け
shared drive
共用ドライブ、
共用駆動装置
shared-equity mortgage
抵当物件エクイティ共有条件貸付け
shareholder
株主
shareholder's equity
自己資本
shares authorized
授権株式数、授権株式
shareware
シェアウェア
shark repellent
企業買収防御策、
会社乗っ取り屋防御策
shark watcher
企業買収対応監視専門家
sheet feeder
シートフィーダー
shell corporation
ペーパーカンパニー、
幽霊会社、架空会社
shift
移る、変動、交替（交代）
shift differential
交代勤務手当
shift key
シフトキー

shift lock
シフトロック
shop
（米）仕事場、作業所、
工場、（英）商店
shopper
買物客、買物代理人
shopping service
ショッピングサービス
short bond
短期債券、短期社債
short covering
買戻し
shortfall
短期投資利益
short form
短文書式、
簡易型
short interest
空売り総額、空売りされたまま買い戻されていない株式
short position
ショートポジション、
売持ち
short-sale rule
空売り規定、
短期見越し売却規定

short squeeze
踏み上げ
short term
短期
short-term capital gain (loss)
短期資本売却収益（損失）

short-term debt or short-term liability
短期国債、短期負債、短期借入金
shrinkage
収縮、縮小（量）、減少
shutdown
一時閉店、操業休止、（工場）閉鎖
shut down (computer)
シャットダウン、遮断
sight draft
一覧払為替手形
sign off
サインオフ
sign on
サインオン
silent partner
匿名社員、裏参加者
silver standard
銀本位制
SIMM (single in-line memory module)
SIMM、シングル・インライン・メモリーモジュール
simple interest
単利
simple trust
単純信託
simple yield
単純利回り
simulation
擬態、模擬実験、シミュレーション
single-entry bookkeeping
単式簿記
single premium life insurance
一時払い保険料生命保険
sinking fund
減債基金、債券償還基金、負債償却積立金
site
用地、現場、所在地
site audit
現場監査
sit down strike
座り込みスト
skill intensive
技術集約的、技術集中的
skill obsolescence
技術老朽化
slack
不振な、不景気な、不活発に
slander
中傷、名誉毀損、悪口
sleeper
スリーパー、後にヒットする商品、大穴
sleeping beauty
眠り姫

slowdown
操短、怠業
slump
スランプ、暴落、景気沈滞
small business
小企業、中小企業
small investor
小投資家、小口投資家
smoke clause
〔保険〕煙害条項
smokestack industry
煙突産業、構造不況産業、
旧技術の既存産業、
重厚長大型の旧式産業
snowballing
雪だるま式に大きくする
（拡大する）
social insurance
社会保険
socialism
社会主義
socially conscious investor
社会意識型投資家
social responsibility
社会的責任
soft currency
軟貨、弱体通貨
soft goods
非耐久財
soft market
軟調市況
soft money
軟貨、紙幣、不換紙幣、
soft spot
弱点、不利な立場
（地位、状態）
soil bank
土壌銀行
sole proprietorship
個人営業、個人店主
solvency
支払能力、弁済能力、資力
source
原因、源泉、利子や配当を
払う人、資料
source evaluation
資料評価
sources of funds
資金源
source worksheet
ソースワークシート
sovereign risk
ソブリンリスク、
国家主権直結機関への信用
供与リスク
space bar
スペースバー
spamming
スパミング、
スパム
span of control
管理限界
special agent
特別捜査官、
特別代理人
special assignment
特別任務、特別割当て、
（財産、権利などの）
特別譲渡
special delivery
速達、速達便、
速達郵便

special drawing rights (SDR)
特別引出権
special handling
特殊取扱い
specialist
専門家、スペシャリスト
special purchase
特別購入
special situation
特別な状況
specialty advertising
特製品
（名産品、特産品）
広告、高級専門品の広告
specialty goods
専門品
specialty retailer
（特選品を扱う）
専門小売店
specialty selling
特選品販売
specialty shop
専門店
sepcial-use permit
特別使用許可
special warranty deed
特別権原担保捺印証書
specie
正金、正貨
specification
(通常 *pl.*）仕様書、
明細（書）、
特許説明書
specific identification
特殊身分証明書
specific performance
〔法律〕特定履行
specific subsidy
特定補助金
speculative risk
投機的リスク
speech recognition
音声認識
speedup
生産増加
spell checker
スペルチェッカー
spending money
小遣銭、現金
spendthrift trust
消費者信託
spider chart
スパイダー図表
spillover
あふれること、過剰、豊富
spin-off
スピンオフ、
副産物
splintered authority
分裂した権威
split
分割する、分配する、
分割、分裂
split commission
分割手数料
split shift
分割勤務、
分割シフト
spokesperson
代弁者、
スポークスパーソン

sponsor
スポンサー、出資者、
保証人、出資する
spot check
無作為抽出検査、
抜き打ち検査
spot commodity
スポット商品、現物商品、
直物商品
spot delivery month
現場渡し（現物渡し、
直渡し）限月
spot market
現金取引市場、現物市場、
スポット市場
spot price
スポット価格、現物価格
spot zoning
スポット地帯制
（地域制、区域制）
spread
広がり、マージン、値開き
spreading agreement
抵当権追加設定契約
spread sheet
スプレッドシート
squatter's rights
不法占拠者の権利、
（土地）
占有者の権利
squeeze
絞めつける、不正手数料、
収賄
stabilization
安定、安定させること、
安定化
stacked column chart
スタックカラム図表、
連続カラム図表
staggered election
ずらし任期選挙、
期差任期選挙
staggering maturities
満期分散
stagnation
停滞、不景気、不振
stake
賭け金、（金銭上、
仕事上の）利害関係、関与
stand-alone system
独立制度、無比のシステム
standard
基準、規範、標準規格品
standard cost
標準原価
standard deduction
標準控除
standard deviation
標準偏差
standard industrial classification (SIC) system
標準産業分類制度
standard of living
生活水準
standard time
標準時、標準時間
standard wage rate
標準賃金率
standby
スタンドバイ、代替物、
交代要員

standby fee
代替物料金、
交替要員手数料、
キャンセル待ち料金
standby loan
準備融資
standing order
継続注文、
継続指図書 **staple stock**
主要株式
start-up
運転（活動、操業）開始、
運転始動、新規事業開始の
start-up screen
スタートアップスクリーン、
始動画面
stated value
表示価格、表記価格
statement
声明、申告、計算書
statement of affairs
業績報告書、資産負債表
statement of condition
貸借対照表、
~条件の明示、
営業報告書
statement of partners' capital
パートナーの資本計算書
static analysis
静態分析、
静学分析
static budget
静態予算
static risk
静態的リスク
statistic
統計の、統計的の、統計値
statistical inference
推測統計、統計的推論、
統計的推理
statistically significant
統計的に重要な
statistical sampling
統計（的）標本抽出
statistics
統計学、統計、統計表
status
地位、資格、情勢
status bar
ステータスバー
status symbol
地位の象徴、身分の象徴、
権威の象徴
statute
制定法、法令、
規則
statute of frauds
詐欺防止法
statute of limitations
出訴期限法
statutory audit
法定監査
statutory merger
法定合併
statutory notice
法定通知期間
statutory voting
法定投票
staying power
持久力、耐久力、
スタミナ

steady-growth method
恒常的成長模型、
均衡成長模型
steering
かじをとる、操縦する、
導く
stepped-up basis
漸増した基準、
向上した基準（標準）
stipend, stipendiary
固定給、俸給、
定期的な支払金
stipulation
合意、条項、
約定
stochastic
確立的な、確立論的な
stock
株式、株式資本、
在庫品
stockbroker
株式仲買人
stock certificate
株券、株式証券
stock dividend
株式配当
stock exchange
株式取引所、
証券取引所、
株式取引
stockholder
株主、家畜所有者
stockholder of record
登録株主
stockholder's derivative action
株主代表訴訟
stockholder's equity
株主持分、自己資本、
純資産、
stock index future
株価指数先物
stock insurance company
株式保険会社
stock jobbing
株の仲買
stock ledger
株式元帳、株式台帳、在庫品元帳
stock market
株式市場、株式取引所、
株式市況
stock option
自社株購入権、
社員持ち株制度、
ストックオプション
stockout cost
品切れ損失
stockpile
備蓄、貯蔵（する）
stock power
株式名義書換委任状、
株式譲渡委任状
stock record
株式元帳、在庫記録
stockroom
貯蔵室、
商品見本展示室、倉庫
stock symbol
株式銘柄

stock turnover
在庫品回転率、
商品回転率
stonewalling
議事妨害、
（調査、投票などを）
意識的に妨害すること、
強固な拒否
stool pigeon
おとりに使うハト、
（警察の）スパイ、
おとり
stop clause
（契約の）終止条項
stop-loss reinsurance
超過損害再保険
stop order
逆指値注文、
差止め命令、
取引停止命令
stop payment
支払停止指図、
支払いを停止する
store
商店、貯える、
保管する
store brand
自社ブランド、
ストアブランド商品
straddle
またぐ、複合オプション、
複合選択付き取引
straight bill of lading
記名式船荷証券、記名式積み荷証券
straight-line method of depreciation
直線法式減価償却、
定額法式減価償却
straight-line production
直線法式生産高
straight time
正規就業時間
straphanger
つり革につかまっている乗客（通勤客）
strategic planning
戦略計画
strategy
戦略、策略、計画
stratified random sampling
層化任意抽出
straw boss
職長代理、監督代行者
straw man
頼りない人、つまらない問題、無資力者、偽証者
street name
〔証券〕仲買人名義
stretchout
引き延ばし、労働強化
strike
ストライキ、同盟罷業、
品質優良
strike benefits
ストライキ手当
strikebreaker
スト破り、スキャップ
strike notice
スト通告、ストライキ通告

strike pay
罷業手当、ストライキ手当
strike price
=STRIKING PRICE 、
権利行使価格
strike vote
スト権確立投票
STRIPS
〔金融〕ストリップ：
（Separate Trading of
Registered Interest and
Principal of Securities)
structural inflation
構造的インフレーション
structural unemployment
構造的失業
structure
構造、組織、建造物
subcontractor
下請負人、下請会社、
下請契約人
subdirectory
サブディレクトリー
subdivider
区分するもの
subdividing
細分すること、
分割すること
subdivision
再分割、一区分、分譲地
subject to mortgage
譲渡抵当に左右される
（に従う）
sublease
（不動産）転貸借
sublet
転貸する、
転貸用の物件
subliminal advertising
サブリミナル広告、
閾下広告
submarginal
限度以下の、必要最低基準
以下の、耕作に適さない
suboptimize
次善の状態にする
subordinated
〔金融〕劣後した、
後順位の、下位におかれた
subordinate debt
劣位弁済債務
subordination
従属関係、債券劣後、
劣後化
subpoena
罰則付き召還令状
subrogation
～の代わりをすること、
代理をすること、
～に代位弁済（請求）する
subroutine
サブルーチン
subscript
下付きの、下付き文字
subscript (computer)
添字、添字をつける
subscripted variable
下付き変数
subscription
寄付申込み、申込み、
株式応募、引受け

subscription price
(株式などの)応募価格、
売り出し価格
subscription privilege
新株引受け特権、
新株応募特権
subscription right
新株引受け権、
（株式の）
優先応募権
subsequent event
続いて起こる出来事
（事件，成行き）
subsidiary
補助の、従属的な、
子会社、同族会社、
subsidiary company
従属会社、子会社、＝
AFFILIATED COMPANY
subsidiary ledger
補助元帳、
subsidy
補助金、
価格調整補給金、
輸出補助金
subsistence
生活、生計費、存在
substitution
取換え、代替、
代用品
substitution effect
代替効果
substitution law
代替調剤法
substitution slope
交替勾配（傾斜）
subtenant
又借り人、転借人、
下級小作人
subtotal
一部分の合計、完全に近い
suggested retail price
提案小売価格
suggestion system
提案制度
suicide clause
自殺条項
suite
スーツ
（パッケージソフト）
summons
呼出状、召喚状、召還令状
sunset industry
斜陽産業
sunset provision
サンセット条項
superfund
スーパーファンド、
有害物質除去基金
superintendent
指導監督者、管理者
supermarket
スーパーマーケット
super now account
スーパーナウアカウント
supersaver fare
特別割引料金
superscript
上付き文字、肩文字、
上添字
super sinker bond
スーパーシンカーボンド

superstore
スーパーストア
supplemental agreement
補足契約書
supplier
供給者
supply
供給する、供給、
供給物
supply price
供給価格
supply-side economics
供給サイド経済、
供給側経済
support level
サポートレベル
surcharge
追加税（金）、追加料金、
付加金、追徴金
surety bond
保証状、
保証書
surge protector
サージプロテクター、
サージ保安器
surplus
超過金、余剰、付加資本
surrender
譲渡する、放棄する、
期限切れ以前に放棄する
surrender, life insurance
生命保険を解約する、
生命保険の解約

surtax
（米）付加税、割増税、
～に付加税を課す
survey
測量する、調査する、
検分する、査察
survey area
測量地域、検分地域
surveyor
測量士、測量技師、検査員
survivorship
生存者への権利の帰属、
生存者財産権、生き残り
suspended trading
保留取引、売買停止
suspense account
仮勘定、未決算勘定
suspension
宙ぶらりんの状態、
一時停止、停止
swap
交換する、（為替を）ス
ワップ取引する、スワップ、
（物々）交換
sweat equity
労働提供、労働出資
sweatshop
労働搾取工場
sweepstakes
賞金レース、総賭け勝負、
投機
sweetener
スイトナー、賄賂
swing shift
（三交代制の）第二次夜勤、
半夜勤、午後交代

switching
切換え、スウィッチ、
むち打ち
symbol bar
シンボルバー、記号バー
sympathetic strike
同情ストライキ
syndicate
企業連合、シンジケート、
公社債募集、引受団体
syndication
シンジケートを結成すること
syndicator
シンジケート運営者
synergy
相乗作用、共力作用
system
系、組織、機構
system (computer)
システム、組織、体系、系
system administrator
システム管理者
systematic risk
体系的リスク
systematic sampling
組織的抽出、系統抽出

T

tab key
タブキー
table column
表の欄,
表のカラム、
目録欄
table field
表のフィールド
T-account
Ｔ字型勘定
tactic
戦法、兵法、
方策
tag sale
ガレージセール
take a bath, take a beating
破産する、
大損する
take a flier
一か八か賭けてみる、
やまを張る、
高飛びする
take a position
買い持ちをする、
ポジションを持つ
take-home pay
（税金などを差し引いた）
手取り賃金（給与）
take
受納する、採用する、
売上高
takeoff
テイクオフ、離陸
take-out loan, take-out financing
〔金融〕テークアウト建設
融資、長期不動産担保金融
takeover
奪取、企業経営権買収、
乗っ取り
taking
取ること、捕獲、売上高
taking delivery
荷取り
taking inventory
在庫品調べ、棚卸し
tally
割賦、割印、一致、
計算
tangible asset
有形資産、有体財産
tangible personal property
有形（有体）個人財産、有
形（有体）人的財産
tank car
タンク車、油槽車、
水槽車

tape
テープ、テープ録音（録画）する、（巻尺で）測る
target audience
対象会衆、大衆、聴衆
target file
目標ファイル
target group index (TGI)
目標（対象）ループ指数
target market
目標市場
target price
目標価格
tariff
関税、関税率、関税表
tariff war
関税戦、関税戦争、
task bar
タスクバー
task force
タスクフォース、特別作業班、特別委員会
task group
任務群、(=TASK FORCE)
task list
タスクリスト
task manager
タスクマネジャー
task management
課業管理
tax
税金、重荷、課税する
tax abatement
減税　（＝ TAX CUT, TAX REDUCTION）
taxable income
課税所得
taxable year
課税年度　（＝ FISCAL YEAR）
tax and loan account
（米）租税国債勘定、租税公債勘定
tax anticipation bill (TAB)
租税準備証券、納税証券
tax anticipation note (TAN)
税収見返り手形
taxation, interest on dividends
配当利子課税
tax base
課税基準、税基盤
tax bracket
税率等級
tax credit
税額控除
tax deductible
課税控除され得る、税控除の
tax deduction
課税控除、課税控除額、租税控除
tax deed
公売証書
tax deferred
課税猶予の、納税猶予の
tax evasion
脱税
tax-exempt property
免税財産、免税資産

tax-exempt security
免税証券
tax foreclosure
税金抵当流れ、
タックスフォークロージャー
tax-free exchange
非課税為替、
免税為替
tax impact
租税効果
tax incentive
税制上の優遇措置、
租税誘引
tax incidence
税負担、租税の帰着
tax lien
租税先取特権
tax loss carryback (carryforward)
租税の損金遡及
（租税の損金繰越）
tax map
租税地図
taxpayer
納税者
tax planning
税金計画、租税計画
tax preference item
税金優先権項目
tax rate
税率、課税率
tax return
納税申告書、税務申告
tax roll
課税台帳
tax sale
滞納処分公売、公売、
兌換処分
tax selling
税金対策として証券売却
tax shelter
タックスシェルター、
税金回避手段
tax stop
税金を止める
tax straddle
税金ストラドル
tax wedge
タックスウェッジ
team building
チーム構築、チーム協力
team management
チーム管理
teaser ad
賞金（賞品）などで購買者の気を引く広告、誘導広告
teaser rate
ティーザーレート、借手誘導のための変動金利モーゲージの導入時のレート
technical analysis
技術的分析
technical rally
（相場の）自律的反発、
人為的回復、
アヤ戻し
technological obsolescence
技術的老朽、
技術的陳腐化
technological nemployment
技術的失業

technology
科学技術、応用技術、
テクノロジー
telecommunications
遠距離通信、
電気通信学
telemarketing
テレマーケティング、
電話による販売・
広告活動
telephone switching
電話交換
template
型板、テンプレート
tenancy
（土地、家屋などの）
保有、占有、
借用権
tenancy at sufferance
黙認不動産権
tenancy at will
任意不動産権
tenancy by the entirety
夫婦全部保有（不動産権）
tenancy for years
定期不動産権
tenancy in common
共有不動産権、共有財産権
tenancy in severalty
単独保有不動産権、
単独保有財産権
tenant
借家人、暫定的不動産権保
有者、貸借人
tenant finish-out allowance
テナント終了引当金
tender
提供（物・する）、入札、
賠償金、請負見積書
tender of delivery
引渡し賠償金
tender offer
株式公開買付け、
テンダーオファー
tenure
保有期間、保有条件、
終身在任権
tenure in land
土地保留期間
term
期間、期限、（*pl.*）
（支払・契約などの）条件
term, amortization
債務償還期限、
債務償還約定日
term certificate
期限付き証券、
定期預金証書
termination benefits
満期給付、満期給付額
term life insurance
定期生命保険
term loan
タームローン
terms
条件、条項、料金
test
試験、を試す
testament
遺言、遺言書、立証
testamentary trust
遺言信託

testate
有効な遺言を残して
testator
遺言者
testcheck
テストチェック
testimonial
証明書（の）、証拠（の）
testimonium
証明、証拠、宣誓証言
test market
テストマーケット、
試験市場、試験販売
test statistic
検定統計
text editing
テキスト編集
text processing
テキスト処理
text wrap
テキストラップ、
テキスト折返し
thin market
閑散な市況、手薄な市況、
薄商い市場
third market
（証券の）第三市場
third party
第三者、第三政党、
サードパーティ
third-party check
第三者小切手
third-party sale
第三者販売
threshold-point ordering
限界点注文
thrift institution
貯蓄金融機関
thrifty
節約する、倹約的な
through rate
スルーレート、通し運賃、
通し値段
tick
目盛、小さな印、点チック
ticker
ティッカー、
株式相場表示板
tie-in promotion
抱き合わせ販売促進、
関連販売促進
tight market
逼迫市場、逼迫市況
tight money
金融引締め、金融逼迫、
金詰まり
tight ship
統制のとれた会社
（組織、機関）
till
(英）レジ、キャッシュド
ローアー、（帳場の）
銭箱
time-and-a-half
５割増の超過勤務手当
time card
就業時間記録カード、
作業時間票
time deposit
有期預金、
定期預金

time draft
一覧後定期払手形、
定期払為替手形、
定期払約束手形
time is of the essence
時間は重要である、
期限厳守
time management
時間管理
time series analysis
タイムシリーズ分析、
時系列分析
time series data
時系列資料、
タイムシリーズデータ
time-sharing
タイムシェアリング
timetable
計画表，時間表、予定表
time value
時間的価値
tip
チップ、警告暗示、
内密の情報
（予想、助言、警告）
title
所有権、権原証書、
敬称、表題
title bar
タイトルバー
title screen
タイトルスクリーン、
タイトル画面
title company
権原保険会社
title defect
権原の欠陥、権原の瑕疵、
権原の欠如
title insurance
権原保険、所有権保証
title report
不動産所有権報告書、
権原報告書
title search
不動産所有権調査
title theory
所有権理論
toggle key
トグルキー
tokenism
名目主義、形式主義
toll
使用料、サービス料、
（通例単数形）
（事後・災害などの）
代償、犠牲者数
tombstone ad
ツームストーン広告、
墓碑広告
toner cartridge
トーナーカートリッジ
tool bar
ツールバー
tool box
ツールボックス
topping out
上げ止まり
tort
不法行為
total capitalization
総資本化、総資産化、

総額資本組入れ
total loss
（保険で）全損
total paid
支払済み総額
total volume
総取引高
touch screen
タッチスクリーン

trace, tracer
跡をつける、複写する、跡、紛失物捜査照会状、転写（透写）用具
trackage
鉄道の総線路、軌道使用料
trackball
トラックボール
tract
地帯、領域、住宅団地、宅地
trade
商業、職業、貿易する、（物々）交換する
trade acceptance
商業引受手形、貿易引受手形、引受荷為替手形
trade advertising
業者向け広告、産業広告、流通広告
trade agreement
貿易協約
trade barrier
貿易障害
trade credit
企業間信用、貿易信用、商業信用状
trade date
取引日、約定日
trade deficit (surplus)
貿易収支の赤字、（貿易収支の黒字）
trade fixture
営業用備品
trade magazine
業界誌
trademark
登録商標、商標、トレードマーク
trade-off
相殺取引、相殺協定、トレードオフ
trade rate
業者間料金
trader
貿易業者、トレーダー、株の売買人、株式証券業
trade secret
企業秘密、営業秘密、取引上の秘密
trade show
商業展示会
trade union
労働組合
trading authorization
取引認可証、取引権限委任書
trading post
貿易所、交易場、銘柄の取引ポスト
trading range
取引限度、値動き幅

trading stamp
商品引換スタンプ、商品券、クーポン券
trading unit
（株式の）取引単位、売買単位
traditional economy
伝統経済
tramp
不定期船、移動労働者、渡り職人
transaction
（業務・交渉・活動などの）執行、取引、売買
transaction cost
取引費用、取引コスト
transfer agent
証券代行、証券代理人、名義書換代理人
transfer development rights
開発権を譲渡する
transfer payment
移転支払、譲渡支払、移転支出
transfer price
移転価格、振替価格、譲渡価格
transfer tax
資産移転税、資産取引税
translate
移す、転換する、外貨に換算する
transmit a virus
ウィルスを送信する
transmittal letter
譲渡状
transnational
超国家的
transportation
運送、輸送手段、交通機関
treason
（国家、政府に対する）大逆（罪）、反逆（罪）、国事犯（罪）
treasurer
会計係、財務部長、財務担当者
tree diagram
樹形図、枝分かれ図
trend
動勢、傾向、トレンド
trend chart
傾向図表
trend line
趨勢線
trespass
不法侵害、立ち入り、不法侵入
trial and error
試行錯誤
trial balance
試算表
trial offer
試供品
trial subscriber
ためし購読者
trigger point
引き金点、トリガーポイント
trigger price
トリガー価格、引き金価格
triple-net lease
三重ネットリース

Trojan horse
トロイの木馬
（破壊的プログラム）
troubled debt restructuring
不良債権の再編成
troubleshooter
調停者、仲裁者、修理係

troubleshooting
傷害解析、
トラブルシューチング
trough
景気の谷
true lease
真正リース
true to scale
目盛どおり、基準どおり、
スケールに一致する
truncation
先端を切ること
trust
信託財産（物件）、
企業連合、信託
trust account
信託勘定
trust certificate
信託証券
trust company
信託会社
trust deed
信託証書
trust, discretionary
裁量信託
trustee
役員、理事、
受託者
trustee in bankruptcy
破産管財人
trust fund
信託資金、信託基金、信託
財産
trust, general management
一般管理投資信託
trustor
信託設定者
truth in lending act
貸付け条件表示制定法
turkey
七面鳥、役に立たない人
（もの）、愚か者
turnaround
一つの仕事（工程、作業）
をやり終えるのに必要な時
間、投資期間、（相場の）
上げ方向への転換
turnaround time
転換時間、投資期間、納期
turnkey
ターンキー方式
turn off
スイッチを切る、
オフにする、消す
turn on
スイッチを入れる、
オンにする、作動させる
turnover
転換、売上高、回転率
twisting
生命保険の乗り換え契約取り、
ツイスティング
two percent rule
２パーセントの法則

two-trailed test
〔統計〕両側検定
***T* statistic**
T統計量
tycoon
巨頭、大立て者、大君（たいくん）

typeface
字形、書体、
タイプフェース
type-over mode
上書きモード

U

umbrella liability insurance
包括的損害賠償保険、
包括的責任保険
unappropriated retained earnings
未処理保留利益、
未処理保留所得
unbalanced growth
不均衡成長、
不均斉成長
unbiased estimator
不偏推定量
uncollected funds
取立未済資金
uncollectible
収集不可能の、
回収できない
unconsolidated subsidiary
非連結子会社
underapplied overhead
過少賦課間接費
undercapitalization
不十分な資本供給、
過少出資
underclass
底辺層、下層階級
underemployed
不完全就業の、
（機械・
設備などが）十分に活用
（利用）されていない
underground economy
アングラ経済、地下経済
underinsured
付保険価額過少の、
一部保険の
underline アンダーライン、
下線、
下線を引く
underlying debt
優先債務、第一債務
underlying mortgage
優位抵当、第一担保
underlying securities
基礎有価証券、原有価証券、
対象有価証券
underpay
（人に）
賃金を十分に払わない
under the counter
不法に取引される（禁制品
など）、内密の、
非合法の
undervalued
過少評価された、価格が減
じられた、軽視された
underwriter
保険業者、証券引受業者

underwriting spread
引受手数料
undiscounted
割引なしの
undivided interest
不可分権
undivided profit
未処理利益、
未配当利益、
未分配利益
undue influence
不当威圧、不適切な影響、
不当な圧力
unearned discount
不労割引
unearned income (revenue)
不労所得　（前受け収益）
unearned increment
（財産、特に土地の）
自然増加、不労増加、
未稼得増加
unearned interest
未経過利子
unearned premium
未経過保険料、
未収保険料、
unemployable
雇用不能な、
雇用に適さない
unemployed labor force
失業労働者
unemployment
失業、失業者数
unencumbered property
抵当に入っていない財産
（不動産）
unexpired cost
未消費原価
unfair competition
不正競争、不公正競争
unfavorable balance of trade
貿易収支の赤字、輸入超過
unfreeze
（資金・予算・施策などの）凍結を解除する
unified estate and gift tax
統一遺産贈与税
unilateral contract
一方的契約、片務契約
unimproved property
改良のない不動産
unincorporated association
法人組織になっていない協会（組合）
unique impairment
一意的損傷、一意的損減
unissued stock
未発行株
unit
一個、構成単位、一定量
unitary elasticity
弾力性１
unit-labor cost
単位労働コスト
unit of trading
売買単位、
取引単位
units-of-production method
（減価償却法での）
生産高比例法

unity of command
命令の統一性
universal life insurance
ユニバーサル生命保険
universal product code (UPC)
（米）統一商品コード
unlisted security
非上場証券
unloading
積荷降ろし、処分、売り抜け
unoccupancy
非居住、非占有、非占有期間
unpaid dividend
未払配当金
unrealized profit (loss)
未実現利益（未実現損失）
unrecorded deed
未登録証書
unrecorded cost
未記録原価
unrecoverable
回復不能の
unsecured debt
無担保負債、無担保債務
unskilled
未熟練の、不熟練の
unwind a trade
逆取引によって証券取引を手仕舞う
update
更新する、書き換える、アップデートする
update (computer)
最新のものにする、アップデートする、改正する
up front
経営陣、先払いとして、原始投下資本として
upgrade
アップグレードする、性能（機能、効果、品質、価値）を高める
upgrade software
ソフトをアップグレードする
upgrading
格上げすること、品質を高めること、効果（性能）を高めること
upkeep
維持、扶養、維持費
upload
アップロード、アップロードする
upper case letter
上段文字、大文字
upright format
アップライトフォーマット、直立様式
upside potential
上限の能力、上昇する可能性
upswing
著しい増加（向上、上昇、発展）

up tick
（需要・供給の）増大、上向き、（事業・景気の）上昇機運
uptrend
（特に経済発展の）上昇傾向、好転、上向き
upwardly mobile
社会的金銭的に上向き移動の、将来有望な
urban
都市の、都会の、都会風の
urban renewal
都市再開発
useful life
耐用年数
user
ユーザー、使用者、利用者
user authorization
ユーザー許可
user manual
ユーザーのための手引き、ユーザーマニュアル
usufructuary right
使用権
usury
高利貸し、高利、法定利率超過利子
utility
有用性、公益事業（電気・ガス・水道などの）、公益事業株（債券）、公共施設
utility easement
公共施設地役権、公益事業地役権
utility program
ユーティリティプログラム

V

vacancy rate
求人率、空き室率
vacant
空の、使用されていない、
無住の
vacant land
空閑地
vacate
（家・部屋・席などを）
明け渡す、空ける、
（職・地位などを）退く
valuable consideration
〔法律〕有価約因、対価
valuable papers (records) insurance
有価証券保険
valuation
（物の）（金銭的）評価、
価値判断、評価額、
生命保険証券の現価評価
value
価値、価格、評価価格
value-added tax 付加価値税
value date
為替資金引渡日
value in exchange
交換価値（＝EXCHANGE VALUE）
value line investment survey
ヴァリューライン投機調査
variable
変わりやすい、変数、可変
variable annuity
変動年金
variable cost
変動費、変動費用
variable interest rate
変動金利
variable life insurance
変額生命保険
variable pricing
変動価格設定
variable-rate mortgage (VRM)
変動金利型抵当
variables sampling
変動見本抽出
variance
変動、差異、分散、齟齬、
適用除外措置
variety store
雑貨店、安物雑貨店
velocity
速度
vendee
買手、買主、引受人

vendor
売手、売主、譲渡人、
自動販売機
vendor's lien
売手先取権、売手留置権
venture
投機、投機の対象になるもの、依託販売積送品
venture capital
危険負担資本、投機資本
venture team
ベンチャーチーム
verbatim
言葉どおりに（の）、
逐語的に）（な）
vertical analysis
垂直分析
vertical discount
垂直割引
vertical management structure
垂直経営層
vertical promotion
垂直昇進
vertical specialization
垂直的分業
vertical union
産業別労働組合（＝INDUSTRIAL UNION）
vested interest
既得権、終身権利、一国の商業や金融活動を支配する人々（団体など）
vesting
受領権、年金付与、
授けられる
vicarious liability
代位責任、使用者責任
vice-president
副大統領、副総裁、副社長
video conference
テレビ会議
video graphics board
ビデオグラフィックス基板
violation
違反、侵害、邪魔
virtual memory
仮想記憶装置
visual interface
ビジュアルインターフェース
vocational guidance
職業指導、就職指導
vocational rehabilitation
職業的復帰
voice mail
音声メール
voice recognition
音声認識
voidable
無（無効、無益）にできる、取消可能な、
〔法律〕無効にできる
volatile
激しく変動する、
揮発性の
volume
量、（しばしば pl.）大量、売上高
volume discount
数量割引

volume merchandise allowance
大量購入割引

voluntary accumulation plan
任意型継続投資プラン

voluntary bankruptcy
自己破産

voluntary conveyance
無償譲渡

voluntary lien
自発的留

voting right
議決権、投票権

voting stock
議決権株、議決権行使株

voting trust certificate
議決権信託証書

voucher
保証人、証拠物件、
証憑書類、伝票

voucher register
支払伝票記入帳

W

wage
（通例 pl.）賃金、給料、報償
wage assignment
給料控除
wage bracket
賃金範囲
wage ceiling
賃金のシーリング設定
wage control
賃金統制
wage floor
最低賃金
wage freeze
賃金凍結
wage incentive
能率給、奨励給
wage-push inflation
賃金インフレーション
wage rate
賃率、賃金率
wage scale
賃金一覧表、賃金階梯表
wage stabilization
賃金安定化
waiver
権利放棄、権利放棄証書
walkout
ストライキをする
wallflower
人気の落ちた銘柄
wallpaper
壁紙
ware
（通例～S）商品、製品
warehouse
倉庫、商品保管所
warm boot/start
ウォームブート
warranty
保証、瑕疵担保責任、保証書
warranty deed
権原担保捺印証書
warranty of habitability
居住性保証
wash sale
仮想売買、なれ合い売買
waste
浪費する、屑、廃棄物
wasting asset
消耗性資産、減耗資産
watch list
要注意人物リスト、警戒事項一覧表
watered stock
水増し株、架空資本

waybill
貨物引換証、貨物送状
weakest link theory
最弱リンク説
weak market
軟弱市況、下向市場
wear and tear
すり切れ、いたみ、磨滅
wearout factor
磨滅要素、損耗要素
web browser
ウェブブラウザー
web server
ウェブサーバー
welfare state
福祉国家
when-issued
(株式・債券が)発効日決済取引の、発効日取引の
whipsawed
〔証券〕二重損をした
white goods
白布製家庭用品、（白く塗った）大型家庭用品、白物
white knight
白馬の騎士、企業買収の危機にある会社を救済するために介入する第三の企業
white paper
白書、公式報告書
whole life insurance
終身生命保険（＝ORDINARY LIFE INSURANCE）
whole loan
全部の貸付
（部分に対して）
wholesaler
卸売業者、卸取次店
widget
小さな機械装置、まだ名のつかないもの、ウィジェット
widow-and-orphan stock
安定配当株
wildcat drilling
無謀な試掘井
wildcat strike
山猫争議、山猫スト
will
意図、遺言書、意思できめる
windfall profit
超過利潤、棚ぼた式利益、意外の利潤
winding up
終了、整理解散、企業閉鎖
window
陳列窓、接触の手段、時間（帯）
window (computer)
ウィンドウ、窓
windows application
ウィンドウズアのプリケーション、ウィンドウズ用アプリケーション
window dressing
（財政などの）粉飾、粉飾勘定、粉飾決算
wipeout
大敗、大破、惨敗

wire house
ワイヤハウス
withdrawal
取消し、撤回、引出した金
withdrawal plan
引出しプラン
withholding
源泉徴収、天引き
withholding tax
源泉徴収税、源泉課税
without recourse
親会社のリスク引受けなし
wizard
ウィザード（プログラム名）、名人
word processing
ワードプロセッシング、文書処理
word wrapping
ワードラップすること
work force
全従業員、全労働人口
working capital
営業資本、運転資本、流動資産
work in progress
仕掛品（＝WORK IN PROCESS）
workload
作業負荷、標準仕事量
work order
製造指図書、工程経路、作業工程
workout
（運動競技の）練習、運動能力適正検査、試験
work permit
就労許可、労働許可
worksheet
作業票、〔会計〕清算表
worksheet (computer)
ワークシート
work simplification
業務簡素化、作業簡素化
work station
ワークステーション
work stoppage
作業停止
work week
週労働日数（時間）
World Bank
世界銀行
world wide web (www)
WWW、ワールドワイドウェブ
WORM
WORM（Write Once, Read Many）(光ディスクの一種)、ワーム
worth
の値打ちがある、有用性、（金銭的な）価値
wraparound mortgage
包括抵当権
wraparound type
循環タイプ、ラップアラウンドタイプ
writ
令状
writer
〔証券〕売り手

write-up
評価増し
writing naked
無約因契約
writ of error
誤審令状
write error
書込み誤り
write-protected
書込み禁止の、
書込みプロテクトの
written-down value
減価償却後価格

XYZ

x-coordinate
X 座標
y-coordinate
Y 座標
year-end
年末（の）、歳末（の）
year-end dividend
年度末配当
year-to-date (YTD)
当会計年度の初めから今日（現在）まで、累計、過去１年間
yellow dog contract
黄犬契約
yellow goods
イエローグッズ（利幅の大きい耐久消費財）
yellow sheets
警察記録（＝RAP SHEET）
yield
産（出）する、譲る、歩留、利回り
yield curve
イールドカーブ、利回曲線
yield equivalence
利回等価、歩留等価
yield spread
利回格差、利回り幅
yield to average life
平均寿命利回り
yield to call
繰上償還利回り
yield-to-maturity (YTM)
満期利回り
yo-yo stock
ヨーヨー株、乱高下する株
zero-base budgeting (ZBB)
ゼロベース予算
zero coupon bond
ゼロクーポン（方式の）割引債券
zero economic growth
ゼロ経済成長
zero lot line
ゼロ敷地線
zero population growth (ZPG)
人口ゼロ成長
zero-sum game
ゼロ和ゲーム
zone of employment
雇用地帯、雇用地域、雇用領域

zoning
区画割の、建築規制、ゾーニング

zoning map
ゾーニングマップ、用途地域図

zoning ordinance
土地利用規制条例

zoom function
ズーム機能

z score
標準得点、ゼロ平均得点